MAGIA SEXUALIS

"I first fell in love with Paschal Beverly Randolph when my eyes had the pleasure of ingesting *Eulis: The History of Love*. The tone of his voice was like a trumpet that kicked up sparks in my soul like listening to John Coltrane. I attempted to acquire all his works, which, one by one, I devoured like a child discovering pudding. But *Magia Sexualis* eluded me in obscurity and exorbitantly priced collector shops. This new translation by Donald Traxler comes at a time when there is much confusion about including consciousness and attention in the sexual act, a time when many are lost in the sexual phantasmagoria of the internet and construct evasive places in their minds to avoid participation with their flesh. The practices contained in this work present an antidote to the disconnection of technology, the detachment of the corporeal, and re-immerse the participant with the act they are engaging in. We can only hope—if people combat and remedy the removal of their souls from the actions of their bodies—it will spread to other areas of all of our lives."

MAJA D'AOUST, WHITE WITCH

"In the field of esoteric studies no one is more mysterious and fascinating than the self-created American original Paschal Beverly Randolph. In this new edition of *Magia Sexualis,* Donald Traxler provides an accurate translation of Randolph's most puzzling and practical text. This text would not have existed but for the synthesizing effort of the European original Maria de Naglowska, under whose hand this work was made manifest. This translation thankfully helps preserve both of these important and obscure figures in our sphere of knowledge."

STEPHEN FLOWERS, PH.D., AUTHOR OF
LORDS OF THE LEFT-HAND PATH

"This undisputable classic of the occultist movement is now available in a reliable English translation. The pioneering importance of Paschal Beverly Randolph has been well known since John Patrick Deveney's great monograph of 1997, but Maria de Naglowska remains largely unknown. *Magia Sexualis* should be an incentive for further investigations into one of the most mysterious personalities in the history of sexuality and its multiple liaisons with esotericism and the occult."

WOUTER HANEGRAAFF, COAUTHOR OF
*HIDDEN INTERCOURSE: EROS AND SEXUALITY
IN THE HISTORY OF WESTERN ESOTERICISM*

MAGIA SEXUALIS

sexual practices for magical power

PASCHAL BEVERLY RANDOLPH
AND MARIA DE NAGLOWSKA

Translated from the French of
Maria de Naglowska
with an Introduction and Notes
by Donald Traxler

Inner Traditions
Rochester, Vermont • Toronto, Canada

Inner Traditions
One Park Street
Rochester, Vermont 05767
www.InnerTraditions.com

Originally published in French in 1931 by Robert Télin under the title
Magia Sexualis

Library of Congress Cataloging-in-Publication Data

Randolph, Paschal Beverly, 1825–1875.
  Magia sexualis : sexual practices for magical power / Paschal Beverly
Randolph ; translated from the French of Maria de Naglowska, with an
introduction and notes, by Donald Traxler.
      p. cm.
  Includes bibliographical references (p.) and index.
  ISBN 978-1-59477-418-8 (pbk.) — ISBN 978-1-59477-507-9 (e-book)
  1. Magic. 2. Sex. I. Naglowska, Maria de, 1883-1936. II. Traxler, Donald.
III. Title.
  BF1623.S4R3613 2012
  133.4'3—dc23

                                                          2012005654

Printed and bound in the United States

10 9 8 7 6 5 4 3

Text design and layout by Priscilla Baker
This book was typeset in Garamond Premier Pro with Democratica and
Avant Garde used as display typefaces

CONTENTS

PART I
THE INTRODUCTORY NOTES

PART II
THE PRINCIPLES

PART III
MAGIC

PART IV
MAGIC MIRRORS

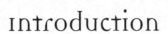

introduction

THE MOST INFLUENTIAL BOOK ABOUT SEX MAGIC EVER WRITTEN

Donald Traxler

There are so many mysteries connected with this book that one hardly knows where to begin in introducing it. *Magia Sexualis* was supposedly written, in English, by Paschal Beverly Randolph. It has, however, only come down to us in French, "translated" by Maria de Naglowska. I have put the word "translated" in quotes because, in reality, Naglowska did much more. Perhaps "compiled" would be a better word. While the greater part of the content can be traced to known works of Randolph, a very significant portion cannot. Our search for answers, for sources, for understanding must begin with these two fascinating and very colorful people.

Paschal Beverly Randolph (1825–1875) may or may not have been, as he claimed, a medical doctor. He did write with apparent easy familiarity about many medical matters, though his opinions hardly represented mainstream thinking, and in at least one case these opinions landed him in jail.*[1]

Randolph may or may not have known Abraham Lincoln. The legend that Lincoln sent him on a diplomatic mission may or may not be true. There is much doubt about these and other points concerning P. B. Randolph. On some other points, though, we are on firmer ground.

What we do know is that Randolph was an occultist, a Rosicrucian, and a sex theorist. He was also a snake-oil salesman who dabbled in the hashish trade.[2] We also know that he finished badly, either by his own hand or that of another, with a gunshot to the head.

From Randolph's own works we know that he wrote in a disorganized and bombastic nineteenth-century style that few, if any, would find acceptable today. If one has read any of Randolph's writings, one is forced to the conclusion that he would not have been capable of producing the clear and well-organized classic that is *Magia Sexualis* in its present form. That, of course, is where Naglowska comes in.

Maria de Naglowska (1883–1936) was born into an aristocratic family in Saint Petersburg. She got the best education a young girl of her time could get and excelled in her studies. Her French was impeccable, and in her later life she is said to have spoken ten languages. She fell in love with a young Jewish musician, Moise Hopenko, and married him, which caused a break with her parents. When her husband, an ardent Zionist, decided to go to Palestine, she was left on her own resources with three small children. She sup-

---

*It was a trumped-up obscenity charge. Randolph spent two days in jail and the case was dismissed.

ported herself by writing, as a journalist, a translator, and a poet. Her writing style in all these forms was spare, clear, and elegant. In addition to her writing skills, Naglowska had many contacts in the world of occultism, and was an occultist herself, with a mystical bent. She eventually gave the world a new religion, which she called the Third Term of the Trinity.

Exactly how Naglowska's partnership with the long-departed Randolph to produce this sex-magic classic came about is not known. She claimed that she had worked from a handwritten manuscript in English, but no such manuscript has ever been found. To add to the mystery, the publisher of *Magia Sexualis,* Robert Télin, claimed on the back cover of the book that the English edition of the work would be forthcoming in December 1931 (just a month after the printing of the French edition). At the same time, French translations of five other works by Randolph were promised. None of this ever came to pass, and it is doubtful whether Naglowska ever translated anything else by Randolph.

So where did this material come from? It gives the impression of having come from an initiatic milieu, and perhaps from more than one such source. Both Randolph and Naglowska had such connections. A close examination of the material reveals that much of it was indeed taken from works by Randolph, such as *The Ansairetic Mystery, The Mysteries of Eulis,* and *Seership! The Magnetic Mirror.* But there is also content there that cannot be found in any of Randolph's known works.* Some of this

---

*One example of this unsourced material is the astrological content, which is not typical of Randolph. It may have come from Naglowska, who had a well-known French astrologer, Jean Carteret, in her magical group, *La Confrérie de la Flèche d'Or.* Similarly, it seems that the material on "volts" and "fluid condensers" cannot be sourced to Randolph's works. Some modern occultists make the facile and perhaps sexist

mystery content may have come from works of his that were never published, or from French Rosicrucians such as Joséphin Péladan, but we must also consider sources that appear to have influenced Naglowska in her own original works, such as Eliphas Levi and Eugene Vintras. Much research remains to be done.*

Whatever its sources, *Magia Sexualis* is the most influential book on sex magic ever written. This is the more amazing, because it was originally published only in French, in an edition of only 1,007 copies.

To be sure, there were other French editions after Naglowska's death. *Magia Sexualis* has also been translated into Italian (by Naglowska's probable lover, Julius Evola), German, Polish, Spanish, and Dutch. In 1988 a pirate edition in English, translated by the late Robert North with the title *Sexual Magic,* was published by Magickal Childe (imprint of the late Herman Slater). I have seen only brief excerpts from North's English translation, and those excerpts contained serious errors. Deveney referred to it as "a translation of sorts,"[3] which is consistent with what I know of North's publications on Naglowska. Even so, the book is now somewhat rare and often sells for as much as a hundred dollars, when it is available.

(cont'd) assumption that Naglowska got this material from Franz Bardon, but they have their chronology, and the direction of the influence, reversed. The first, German, edition of Bardon's book, *Initiation Into Hermetics* (see bibliography), was published in 1956, twenty years after Naglowska's death. *Magia Sexualis* was published in 1931, when Bardon was in his very early twenties.

*There is a claim that the ritual part of *Magia Sexualis* was taken from the ritual part of Péladan's novel, *À Coeur perdu* (see bibliography). I have not found the evidence and remain skeptical. Naglowska does share some symbolism with Eliphas Levi, but other sources are possible, especially since the symbolism is Masonic. Vintras seems to have influenced Naglowska's original works, but not necessarily *Magia Sexualis*. More work remains to be done.

Bearing all of the above in mind, and having a special interest in Maria de Naglowska, in addition to my interest in Randolph, it seemed to me that a good edition in English was much needed. It is my hope that the present translation will fill that need and that in this form *Magia Sexualis* will achieve greater renown than ever before.

DONALD TRAXLER began working as a professional translator (Benemann Translation Service, Berlitz Translation Service) in 1963. Later he did translations for several institutions in the financial sector. On his own time he translated poetry and did his first metaphysical translations in the early 1980s. He later combined these interests, embarking on an ambitious, multiyear project to translate the works of Lalla (also known as Lalleshvari, or Lal Ded), a beloved fourteenth-century poet of Kashmir Shaivism. That project is still not complete, but many of the translations have become favorites of contemporary leaders of the sect. He is currently focusing on Western mysticism in a five-book series on Maria de Naglowska for Inner Traditions. He is contemplating a major project on another European mystic and an eventual return to and completion of the Lalla project. Except for Lalla, he translates from Spanish, French, and Italian. All of his projects are labors of love.

magia sexualis

preface

AN INSTRUMENT OF INITIATIC KNOWLEDGE

PASCHAL BEVERLY RANDOLPH

Doctor Paschal Beverly Randolph* is one of the great, mysterious figures of nineteenth-century occultism.

There has been much talk about him, and much heated discussion of his bizarre theories by those not initiated into them, outside of his students and secret adepts. But it has never been possible to reconstruct the personality and intimate life of this American mulatto who trusted no one and constantly surrounded himself with absolutely impenetrable mystery. Silence was his emblem and the watchword that he imposed on all those who approached him.

Still, the few details, furnished by some of his friends, attest that this man, possessed of an unusual strength of will and a tenacious perseverance, completely mixed his personal life with the work to which he had consecrated himself from his youth. He had only one goal and never withheld from it the smallest bit of his energy: to

---

*[Naglowska spelled this name as "Pascal Bewerly Randolph." —*Trans.*]

know the supreme laws of Life and of the Creation by means of continual study and experience.

Randolph's life was, indeed, an effort of uninterrupted discipline with a view to becoming the instrument of initiatic knowledge that he wished to be.

Randolph was the first who fearlessly raised the veil covering the nudity of Isis, and this immense courage allowed him to proudly proclaim that the key to all the mysteries of the Universe is to be found in Sex.

"Sex is the greatest magical power of Nature," Randolph said, and he demonstrated it to his students.

Randolph had begun his studies in the heart of the secret society known as the H. B. of L. (Hermetic Brotherhood of Luxor), whose headquarters were located in Boston on Boylston Street. But, in about the year 1870, he founded his own initiation circle, E. B. (Eulis Brotherhood), and, together with the doctors Fontaine and Bergevin, he examined occult data in the light of contemporary science.

Barbet, who was one of his best friends, was amazed by the results obtained: the mysterious, the incomprehensible, were boldly brought to the state of clear truths, controlled by strict laboratory procedures.

This was a true revolution in the occultists' world, for it took away the most redoubtable weapon of the merchants of mystery while at the same time bringing to nothing their dubious methods of enrichment at the expense of gullible crowds.

With science supporting and controlling the miracle, the latter became a concrete reality under certain well-determined conditions, but it looked like humbug and lying when those conditions were not fulfilled.

A ferocious campaign was then directed at Randolph. He was accused of having betrayed the traditions, of having revealed the key of the mystery, reserved for the initiates, of having thrown pearls before swine.

Madame H.-P. Blavatsky fought him violently. Between her and him there was one of those spiritual wars of which we have an example in the well-known case of the conflict between Peladan and Eliphas Levi.

The founder of the Theosophical Society unleashed a sort of occult duel against Randolph, which caused, they say, the premature death of the latter.

But all this agitation, visible and invisible, around the name and work of Randolph made him famous, if not rich. His novels were read and commented upon, although often in a contradictory manner. His *Asrotis,* his *Dhoula-Bell,* his *Magh-Thesor,* his *She,* and his *Master Passion,* knew their hour of glory, while his theoretical treatises, such as *The Magnetic Mirror, The Ansairetic Mystery, Communication with the Dead,* and *The Intimate Secrets of the Mysteries of Eulis,* got the passionate attention of specialists.*

Still, in all the books, light was not shed completely. P. B. Randolph—who in spite of what his detractors said, did not throw pearls before swine, knowing the dangers of too hasty revealing— kept the definitive keys for complete understanding of his work for the members of his circle, the Eulis Brotherhood.

---

*[Of the titles that Naglowska mentioned, *Asrotis, Magh-Thesor,* and *She* are unknown. *Dhoula-Bel* was the title of the German translation of Randolph's "Rosicrucian novel," *Ravalette,* published by Gustav Meyrink in 1922. —*Trans.*]

The volume that we offer to the reader today contains some of these keys: magical abstracts and recipes accompanied by explanatory notes, which Randolph's disciples transcribed in their own handwriting, from the Master's dictation.

These fragments, infinitely precious because formidably efficacious, have in addition been supplemented by some chapters, taken on the one hand from the theoretical part of the *Intimate Secrets of the Mysteries of Eulis* and on the other from *The Magnetic Mirror*, notably from the introduction to this work and from its practical part, which has still never been published.

In delivering these keys to the cultivated public of our time, we declare ourselves to be the defenders of Randolph's work, while rejecting the stupid accusation of black magic.

And anyway, what do those two words mean, that even today so many not-very-enlightened persons pronounce with fear? Nothing, except a superstitious fear, remains of a long period of somber ignorance.

Magic is a science that differs from the so-called positive sciences due to the psychic and spiritual factors, which it implies just as well for the object as for the subject of the operative act. Magic is never either white or black; but it can be benefic or malefic, according to the purpose for which one makes use of it. Magic is a weapon, and like all weapons, one can make use of it for the good or ill of oneself or another—but because it is powerful, it is obviously dangerous in unskillful hands.

But magic is also a sacred and royal science in the sense that it cannot be acquired by someone who is not worthy of it; and morbid neuroses and often even madness are the share of those who give themselves to it without the requisite aptitude and preparation.

Paschal Beverly Randolph

It is necessary to be armed with patience, with calm, and with a great courage to clear its first threshold, and above all, it is necessary to love this science for itself, and not for the material and personal advantages that it procures.

P. B. Randolph had these qualities and still more; that is why he became a great magician, whom all vaguely feared and envied. If he died young, while his adversary, Madame H.-P. Blavatsky, triumphantly lived to a very advanced age, it is, undoubtedly, because his task on this earth was finished more rapidly than that of the founder of the theosophical movement.

For, indeed, Randolph's mission was to find and to temporarily hide a light; that of H.-P. Blavatsky was to train the masses.

Today those masses are trained, and they will accept and understand without too much trouble the things that, in 1880, would have done them more harm than good.

The modern spiritualist elite will line up on the side of Randolph, without failing to recognize, because of that, the indisputably magnificent work of H.-P. Blavatsky, whose memory we here respectfully salute.

Each epoch has its task, and its recognized personage.

MARIA DE NAGLOWSKA

PART I

the
introductory
notes

INTRODUCTION TO THE MYSTERIES

I n some of our publications—which have created some discontent, and even an offensive movement against us among the occultists, who cannot admit the Sacred Doctrine that we teach, in confrontation with the one that they have forged, perhaps the more comfortably to navigate there—we have brought into relief the principal laws, the true fundamentals that every initiate discovers one day, no matter what path he has followed.

We have summarized these truths in a series of manuscript volumes, proclaiming from the first page that *the principal and greatest force of Nature is Sex.*

The Brotherhood of Eulis, which was the first to recognize and accept this truth, knew to what attacks it was exposing itself by this act. But, scorning the enemy, it entrusted our manuscript to some trustworthy persons, repeating to them the ancient recommendation not to *cast pearls before swine.*

Unfortunately, the book passed thus into other hands.

It is quite regrettable, for the path that we follow is a royal path, which is not made for imbeciles and charlatans, nor for recipe-seekers with egotistical aims.

This path is reserved for courageous men and for those rare women who know how to apply it usefully. In the book titled *The Mysteries of Eulis** we have indicated some material means that can serve as directives to avoid morbid psychic states; but all of that can only be useful for individuals, mentally strong, because the higher powers are only given to those who are able to appreciate them. These forces never come to rest in the great emptiness of weak souls, and they do not reveal themselves to a man except when the various currents of exterior influences have become calm in him, thanks to his cool and patient will, ritually tested.

The Brotherhood of Eulis wishes to make of each of its students an independent individuality; that is why it lets them work freely on perfecting themselves, giving them only a general method and some pieces of good advice based on experience.

When the brotherhood gives its instruction book to someone it doesn't believe that he is ready to understand the doctrines. The book is only a path, drawn according to a plan: the student himself must raise the sail of his ship and steer with his own hand toward the shore where the sun shines.

The student who accepts our directives learns how to exercise "volantia," "decretism," and "posism,"† helped by material means that facilitate the work and give the keys to the acquisition of a force

---

*[This work, apparently intended for his more advanced students, was never printed by Randolph. It has only survived in one manuscript, which was purchased by John Yarker from Randolph's widow. It is now most easily accessible as appendix B to Deveney's book (see bibliography). —*Trans.*]

†[These three techniques are fundamental to Randolph's system. They are elucidated in chapters 5, 6, and 7. —*Trans.*]

that brings, according to the case, blessing or damnation, with lightning rapidity.

This force is similar to that which furiously unchains the elements of nature, but the initiate, warned and wise, masters them triumphantly.

THE FAITH OF EULIS

Everything on Earth, physical or metaphysical, every force, every quality or power of the Universe, has its center, its cycle, and its seasons.

It is necessary to put oneself in harmony with this universal regime if one does not wish to succumb.

There are spheres, evolving in space, from which emanate strictly determined influences.

They are inhabited by intelligences, fluid and solid, and by forces, which a man can direct and with which he must wish to unite himself if he knows the law of agreements between matter and spirit.

Chance does not exist. In human life, just as in the whole Universe, every fact or event is the result of causes and rules, governing the world for endless time. This is certainly what permits divination.

The Brotherhood of Eulis believes in the great and intelligent Presence, in the Power and in the Strength, in which the past, the present, and the future are totally reflected.

This Presence is surrounded by beautiful mental energies, and formidable powers envelop its Supreme Essence.

The Brotherhood of Eulis believes in the electric, etheric, and fluid worlds situated beyond the borders of the material world.

The correspondence with these worlds is subject to the laws of Nature, and one discovers them near the fluid isles, around which they float like eggshells, on the swollen breasts of the Azure Sea.

These worlds are more beautiful, grander, more mysterious than our widest terrestrial horizons.

They extend toward the infinite, populated by resplendent beauties, decorated with immense clouds and constellations; and they form, through vast spaces, boundless landscapes.

These worlds are to our universe as the latter would be to a city of termites in the jungles of Africa.*

The Brotherhood of Eulis believes in the great armies of beings and powerful intelligences whose origin is neither human nor material, and compared to which the most sublime genius of Earth is no more than a very small grain of sand on a majestic mountainside, a drop of water in the immense ocean, a weak breeze carried by the hurricane that rages above the celestial landscapes.

The Brotherhood of Eulis believes in the reality of these worlds, invisible to the ordinary eye, because its initiates have gazed upon them in their *sialam*† exaltations.

These initiates have testified that these worlds do not originate with our Earth, nor from any other world similar to our own.

The beings who inhabit them know the higher mysteries, and they proclaim that the true power of the spirit is acquired in

---

*[This comparison is from Randolph, in *The Mysteries of Eulis,* and not from Naglowska. —*Trans.*]

†[This term, used by both Randolph and Madame Blavatsky, refers to a trance-sleep, sometimes associated with the use of magic mirrors. —*Trans.*]

conjunction with the power of sex, because the two elements are complementary one with the other.

But one cannot establish rapport with these entities by means of the methods of the spiritualist circles, nor through hypnotism, and customary intellectual means are not of any help in this.

Only the sialam trance (a Tibetan method) permits one to evoke their images, by means of the magic mirror, for they are supra-human spirits, intelligences, wisdom, and energies.

They are called "Neridii," and the philosophy they teach is called "the philosophy of Eulis."

We, the members of the Brotherhood of Eulis, believe in God, recognizing His omniscience and omnipresence, and we also believe that Man has been created in His image.

We believe in Nature, which is for us the manifestation of the Supreme Intelligence, and we proclaim that God resides everywhere and in each of us.

And in contemplating Nature in its multiple and diverse manifestations, in basing ourselves on our personal experience, and in letting ourselves be guided by the wisdom that has been revealed to us, we affirm that Sex is the principal and fundamental force in every being, the most powerful force in Nature, the most characteristic evidence of God.

3

THE POLARIZATION
OF THE SEXES

T he mysteries dealt with in this work carry the names
"Mysteries of Eulis" and "Ansairetic Mysteries."

The Mysteries of Eulis, containing the theory based on the
supreme laws, is placed before us as the science of the higher spheres,
while the Ansairetic Mysteries are its application in the material
sphere.*[1]

The application of the theoretical elements envisaged in the
"Mysteries of Eulis" finds its key in the strict and universal law of
polarizations, which is at the same time the foundation upon which
rests the whole inspired edifice of the doctrine of Eulis.

---

*[These two rather short works would have been circulated only privately during
Randolph's lifetime. A version of the "Ansairetic Mysteries" was included in the supplement to *The New Mola!* (see bibliography), where it appears on pp. 65 *ff.* This
version in the supplement includes a set of rules, #17 of which is prefixed by the
following: "[Note: At this stage the *esoteric points* of the mysteries come in. They are
never printed, but are written to such as need and will properly observe them . . .]"
The rule that follows begins with three dots, indicating that something has been
left out. According to Deveney, the rule originally referred to hashish. It should be
noted that this version of the "Ansairetic Mysteries" is not the same as the document
called "The Ansairetic Mystery" that appears in Deveney's book (see bibliography) as
appendix A. —*Trans.*]

Indeed, the whole universe, all living beings, without the least exception, are ruled by the principle of two contrary forces, the one exercising upon the other an unavoidable power of attraction. They are called the positive and negative forces, and one finds them in good and evil, emission and reception, life and death, idea and action, man and woman (positive and negative magnetic poles) on the material plane, and, just the opposite, woman (active pole) and man (negative pole) on the mental plane.

The science of the mysteries teaches us that, just as in nature the sex of the male attracts the sex of the female, we can attract to ourselves the desired form by creating the negative, that is, its opposite.

That is the basic principle of all magic; no law is superior to it, and it allows us to accomplish the operative acts in two ways: intellectually, that is to say, coldly, without joy, and sensually, that is to say, in love.

No one is unaware that the greatest miracle of Nature is the procreation of the species. It is the materialization of energy flashing forth from the union of two opposite poles: the positive and the negative. But, in the sexual union of a man with a woman, the contact is established not only on the physical plane but also on the mental plane for, as the law of Hermes states, "that which is below is like that which is above."

Now, while the phallus of the man is polarized positively and the kteis of the woman negatively, the head of the man, the organ of his mental manifestations, is, on the contrary, negative with respect to the head of the woman, which is positive.

This explains why the man, full of initiative in what concerns the physical manifestations of love, waits for the invitation of the

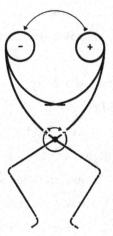

Fig. 3.1. The polarization of the sexes

woman, her feeling and her mental passion, to climb the ladder of union on the higher planes.

Before the physical joining (*in the normal case, it should be understood*) all of the senses of the man and of the woman are brought into play so that the mental idea may be able to become fixed under the best conditions, in conformity with the law of induction between the mental and physical poles of the two individuals of different sex.

This phenomenon, known for thousands of years, is found to be at the base of the mystery called *Mahi Caligna,** whose laws essentially come down to this:

1. The mental current (a) is at its paroxysm at the moment of ejaculation, in the man as well as in the woman.

---

*[Naglowska spelled this as "Mahi Kaligua," which suggests that she may indeed have been working from a handwritten manuscript rather than from a printed text. Randolph, with his facility for neologisms, defined it as "the Sexive principle of Eulis."
—*Trans.*]

2. Under certain well-determined conditions, one can make use of this current to influence the laws in their most distant manifestations.

3. By its induction upon the material sphere, one obtains the causes of the desired effects.

4. Thoughts, ideas, penchants, and individual origins leave their impression during coitus, in the astral sphere. These impressions do not make themselves known until later and do not always reveal the hereditary qualities of the individual. Still, they always act upon the events and actions of the astral spheres.

THE MAGICAL CHAIN
AND ITS DIVINITIES

The arcana dealt with in the preceding chapter are brought together under the title of *Mahi Caligna,* that is to say, *the science of the ancient age,* because the generations that preceded us knew them and cultivated them.

We venture to affirm that because we ourselves have received them by *tradition,* and because we find testimonial to them in fabled monuments, erected in honor of the divinities of ancient Egypt, in the thrusting lines of the obelisks, which rise up to the blue sky like fecund phalli of the sandy flatlands.

This evidence teaches us that the sacred law of love rules not only the earth but also the whole universe.

We find its revelation in Asia, in the sculpted images of divinities, whose arms, raised to heaven to bless or to terrify, attest to the truth of our doctrines and symbolize the power of the holy connections of love.

Besides, whatever one may say about it, the phallic truth is at the base of all the rituals of the secret societies, and the sacred art and the holy scriptures of all nations speak its mystery to those who know how to read them.

The hierophants of ancient Egypt knew the suggestive power of art. That is why they made it subservient to religion, imposing strictly determined laws and means of expression on the sculptors and painters.

It was a great benefit to humanity, for, impregnated with certain truths, thanks to the images and to the prayers, constantly seen and heard, the believers realized them automatically in their sexual couplings. And in this way, utilizing the creative energy of all the couples, the priests really populated the astral sphere with divinities and demiurges, nourished, in addition, by the vital power of the imagination of the masses. The people's astral group thus became powerful.

For love, divine force, endlessly creating, by the joining together of the positive and negative atoms, was nourished by the mystic exaltation or by the fright of the masses, prostrated before the altar; and the latter became, through the generations, the vase where the forces gathered, which brought, according to the will of the one commanding, good or ill, light or shadow, life or destruction.

Love is the only universal law, which rules the infinite spaces and deploys an irresistible action everywhere that life reigns, and a people among whom the nuptial practices are always in conformity with the eternal laws constitutes a great magical chain, binding the material sphere to the higher spheres.

From that there results an alliance of human forces with divine or spiritual forces, and the intelligence of Man then acquires the possibility of dominating both here and there. Mankind becomes the master of good and evil and makes use of it according to his will.

This is the principle and the truth that, under such conditions

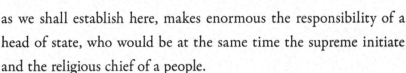

as we shall establish here, makes enormous the responsibility of a head of state, who would be at the same time the supreme initiate and the religious chief of a people.

But, on the other hand, when religion is effaced and humanity forgets the primordial truths that we are reestablishing here, and gives itself blind shepherds, the evils that fall upon nations are greater still.

And when the anger accumulated in the higher spheres is unfurled upon the earth, because of the injustice and licentiousness of human life, no man has the power to stop the scourges and to master the storms that destroy the world.

These are the critical periods in the history of humanity, and each race has had its part in it.

PART II

the principles

5

"VOLANTIA" (SIGN A)

Every student who proposes to penetrate the mysteries of Eulis and the ansairetic mysteries must, first of all, learn to master himself in all circumstances in order to advance upon the path of wisdom as a master and not as a slave.

He must search, beyond that, to constantly enlarge his intellectual horizon and his forces of individual action: the mental forces, the magnetic forces, the psychic forces.

The student must learn to exercise his diverse capacities and his will in a calm fashion, without nervous exhaustion.

This is what we call *volantia*.

We find its model in the irresistible force of the thunderbolt, which breaks and burns but does not tire.

The student must develop in himself this elementary force—volantia—which is passive, for it obeys the command of the intellect, and cold, for it is exempt from all passion.

This force must be developed and strengthened through a mechanical procedure in order that no emotionalism should influ-

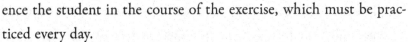

ence the student in the course of the exercise, which must be practiced every day.

One should fasten to the wall a white disk with a black center.

One should stare at the black center of the disk for sixty seconds, remaining perfectly still.

That will strengthen the student's capacity for concentration, as well as his attention.

When the prescribed minute has run out, one should turn the face—without changing the position of the eyes—toward a white surface, upon which the optical illusion will make us see the same disk, but with reversed colors: the background black, the center white.

The illusory vision will disappear some seconds later and will be repeated again if one remains motionless.

One must see the disk that is due to the optical illusion four times and, later, seven times.

When the student has become familiar with this first exercise he shall repeat it with other disks, according to the spectrum of colors in the rainbow. He will thus develop these three capacities: attention, concentration, and attraction.

Five or six months later—if he practices methodically every day—the student will have acquired the capacity to create, while calmly staring at a white surface, a mental form, which will attract the corresponding astral body. This body will solidify itself before the student, and communication between the two will be established.

The same exercise can be done with the help of a magic mirror in the middle of which a small, white disk has been pasted.

The desired effect is thus obtained more easily and more quickly: a figure suddenly forms on the polished surface of the mirror, and this figure looks at you as if to question you.

There is no danger attached to this type of phenomenon, but there are some students who cannot bear such visions. We advise those students to not persevere and to abandon this first step on the path to magic, for sensitivity that degenerates into fear is a sign of weakness. Only the strong should and can advance.

For an exercise period of thirty days we prepare the disks in the following manner: we sink three nails into the center of the disk at a distance of an inch from each other. The first nail is zinc, the second is copper, the third is iron.

We surround the nails with a wire of copper or zinc, one end of which is held in the right hand.

One stares at the middle of the disk, while remaining completely motionless.

By this means one gets the help of electricity, which consolidates the attention and favors the quality of the concentration, while making it more positive.

It is necessary to repeat this exercise for a period of three to eight months before being able to operate with metaphysical goals.

The exercises intended to develop volantia, just as those that we describe further on for the development of decretism and posism, must be done with the greatest care and in an attitude of perfect seriousness, for the least straying from the magical way provokes neuroses, often incurable.

We repeat: do not persevere if you experience fear and mental distress.

6

"DECRETISM"

The second principle of power that the student of magic must acquire carries, among us, the name of *decretism*.

It is the capacity to give inescapable orders, to impart desires, thoughts, and feelings to another, and to provoke verbal declarations, and so forth.

It is also the power to create entities, capable of living, moving, appearing and disappearing, getting up, falling down, stopping, and flying, as we command them.

It is the dictatorial quality, the positive power of the human being, without which one can't do anything real, either for good or for ill.

It is very important that at the instant of giving the order, the imagination of the orderer should be absolutely free of every other preoccupation, and that no emotion should creep in to influence the command, which takes off then like a bolt of lightning, traverses whatever amount of space, and, in crossing the oceans and deserts, infallibly comes to rest upon the designated target: a living being or an inert object.

The duration of the command's flight, from its point of

departure to the point of arrival, does not exceed three to seven seconds.

It is the benefic or malefic energy of the human soul.

It is also the most formidable force of Man, which can be employed either for good or ill.

Therein lies its danger.

This force is subject to some laws of periodicity; the curve that it follows is elliptical; and its nature is magnetic.

This explains, among other things, why the sender of the orders feels their counterstrike, in the sense that the good or ill that he provokes infallibly falls back upon himself.

The evil that a powerful decretist can do is the greater accordingly as his feelings are more improper; that is why we do not admit into our schools those individuals who have a habit of lying, who babble too much, who often devote themselves to unrealizable projects, or who are weak or disturbed in their nerves.

In addition, we advise our students to first test their decretism force on themselves and to only go on to decretism with regard to others after long experience and real purification of soul.

There are no special exercises for developing decretism. This force manifests itself naturally in the subject who is victorious in the tests of volantia, and it grows progressively with use.

7

"POSISM" (SIGN S)

The third principle of power that the adepts of our doctrines develop in themselves is *posism,* that is to say, the realization of the receiving or sending state by means of the special position of the body and of its particular zodiacal orientation, accompanied by a propitious state of idea and sentiment.

It is, to summarize, the science of gesture, very difficult to acquire, but whose results are among the most important.

To obtain this power, it is indispensable to first develop the attention and the capacities of concentration and abstraction, just as in the cases of volantia and decretism, which have been discussed in the preceding chapters.

An adept, expert in posism, when he wants to give or receive a stroke, a kiss, or a caress, *poses,* that is to say, places his body in a certain way and gives to his face the necessary expression, by means of the look, the nostrils, and the mouth, exactly as does an actor on the stage.

He chases from his spirit every imagination or preoccupation that is foreign to his purpose and awaits the desired realization, which is accomplished by virtue of the law according to which everything that is *realized* on the higher planes—metaphysical, mental, and etheric—of a being is equally reproduced on the physical plane, and vice versa.

It is easy to understand that the difficulty consists above all in the total concentration of spirit solely on the effect desired, for what characterizes the habitual human state is precisely the simultaneity of the most diverse thoughts.

That is why in certain lodges the students practice posism for years before proving their capacity in this sense.

To practice posism, it is necessary to conform oneself to the following rules.

1. Choose for the exercise (once for all) a peaceful room, where no exterior noise gets in and where strangers never penetrate.

2. Study in front of a mirror the most suitable position and expression for the sending or receiving of the desired idea.

3. Do not devote, in the beginning, more than five minutes, at the most, to the posism exercise, in order to not take on harmful habits, which could cause fatigue provoked by the excess of effort. A month later, even a minute will suffice. Always exercise at the same hour.

4. For an idea to become *posist,* that is to say, apt for realization following the *pose,* as it is described above, it must be held without a second of relaxation, until it becomes *customary* to your mental being.

This cannot, of course, manifest itself in the first days of exercise.

Often, several weeks are not even sufficient; but with perseverance, one will certainly get there.

When the desired result is obtained, that is to say, when the idea that you *pose* has become customary to your mental being, in which it is, consequently, realized, its delivery, or material realization, is obtained instantly, and the sender knows it infallibly.

It is difficult to explain to one unschooled by which precise sensation he will recognize the habituation achieved in the mental sphere; still, the poet knows something about it, for this sensation is close to what one could call the life, in the soul of the poet, of the landscapes and persons imagined.

But it isn't necessary to know in advance what this sensation will be like: persevere, and you will know it.

5. The principal *poses,* which it is necessary to study, are the following:

   a) *For passive reception:* Kneel down; sit on your heels; bend your arms at a right angle, resting your elbows on your legs; bring your forearms up slowly, without moving your elbows, until you are touching your shoulders with the backs of your hands. The fingers must be slightly curved, in such a way that their ends are in the same plane. Bend the torso back a little and stay immobile, observing all the general indications given above.

   b) *Pose of active passions:* Crouch on the ground, bending a little forward. Extend your arms, slightly bent at the elbows, and imitate the claws of an eagle with your hands, the palms turned forward. As a theme for practice you can choose anger, at first personal with a chosen subject, then personal without a subject. Later you will *pose* general (abstract) anger with a chosen subject, and finally abstract anger without a subject.

Each of these themes must be studied separately for a period of at least a month.

At the end of the whole series of these exercises, one will know what pure anger is and in what way it partakes of the nature of a storm. This knowledge is very important for the occultist who seeks to penetrate into the essence of the cosmic elements with a view to uncovering their laws and life in human beings.

Later still, one will repeat the same exercises to know the essence, more distant from us, of abstract goodness, which has nothing in common with our *charity,* and after all that one will attempt to penetrate the *truth* of love. Once one knows all these things, one will try, always according to the same method, to know justice.

He who knows justice will have gained enormously on the path of evolution, for he will have the key to balance, upon which rest all the static and dynamic laws of life.

The primordial and derived knowledge that one acquires in submitting oneself to the regime of our methods is completely different from that given by books, for it places the student in the real essence of things, while books only teach the relationships between postulated ideas.

Cerebral study (*which at the same time must not be neglected*) confers the memory of words and teaches the art of juggling them; but our methods, which rest upon the ancient wisdom of Africa and Asia, give real knowledge of what is.

c) *For active sending:* Sit on the ground, legs crossed. Extend your arms forward, palms turned toward the ground. From shoulder to fingertips your arms should form a single straight line.

d) *For passive sending:* Sit as in *c*, or remain standing, placing the right foot one step forward. Slowly spread your arms, bending them slightly at the elbows, and form your hands like two vessels able to hold a globe. Raise your arms, without at all changing the form given to your hands, up to forty-five degrees above the level of your shoulders.

e) *Aspiration:* Extend yourself on a flat surface, facing the ceiling. Open your arms, palms open, and make an angle of forty-five degrees with your extended legs. This position calms the flesh and the nerves and permits the body to draw in new forces, spread through the atmosphere that surrounds you and through the more distant regions, visible and hidden.

f) *Isolation for defense:* Sit on the ground. Bend your knees and bring them close to your forehead. Put your arms around your legs, and interlace your fingers.

g) *Active isolation:* Lie on your back. Put your right leg over your left and interlace your fingers over your stomach, the backs of your hands turned up normally. Spread your thumbs and little fingers a bit, and make the tips of them touch. If you do this pose well, you will soon feel a warm current in your hands.

6. The passive positions are intended, for the most part, for operations whose goal is the reception of a force. The active positions we ourselves send out, on the other hand, are gestures of aggression or of defense.

7. The experienced *posist* makes use of his faculties, developed by the means that we have just indicated, to prepare himself for certain environments, for meeting certain persons, or in general for entering into contact with whatever type of living being, with a view to penetrating his particular mental state or to guess his next action in certain special situations.

Further, by means of *posism* one can, at will, attract qualities, good or bad, that one does not as yet possess, but of which one has need for influencing others.

Quite a few of the rites of secret societies and even of official religions are based on the science of posism.

In any case, a student beginning the posism exercises need not concern himself with what has just been summarized in 7. We are only referring to the uses that are inherent to our work, and we only give these notes for information's sake.

We recommend that students not forget that posism is not only a gesture of the body, which would be limited to it. The gesture by itself would be nothing, if it did not give rise to a corresponding mental state. Every gesture creates a thought, and every thought is an influence.

But it is further necessary to understand the essential difference that separates thought from word. A word is anemic; a thought is full of blood. A word has a dull resonance; a thought vibrates like metal. A word is a static image; a thought is a dynamic being.

The gesture gives rise to a thought, which acts even before it has been clothed in words.

Posism awakens thought, not word.

8

"TIRAUCLAIRISM"

*Tirauclairism,** or the power of evocation, which permits communication with those who are absent, the dead, and invisible entities, is very difficult to exercise.

Nighttime lends itself best to this kind of operation because of its relative calm; but many months of patience are necessary, and sometimes even years, to acquire, in this sense, a sufficient capacity.

We give beginners the following advice.

Fix in your mind an image or a flash of light, and do not be distracted from it.

Concentrate your attention upon this image or this light, and firmly protect yourself from all other images and from the phantoms that will seek to capture your spirit at this moment.

It will be impossible for you to practice higher magic if you do not first develop, if you do not reinforce thereafter, in yourself, the royal faculty of tirauclairism, which will make you the master of your mind.

The common person is a slave of the fragments of images and thoughts that pass like a chaotic crowd through his disorganized brain.

Be the lord of your faculties, acquired or reorganized by you, and

*[This word was spelled as "tirau-clairism" by Randolph. I have retained Naglowska's nonhyphenated form, as it makes more sense to me. —*Trans.*]

you will then be able—then only!—to evoke the hierarchies that preside and personify the great human qualities (knowledge, wisdom, loyalty, sincerity, courage, mercy, justice, logic, poetry, magic) that are reflected in the different branches of human learning (geometry, hygiene, dialectic, psychology and philosophy, war, medicine, jurisprudence, music, astronomy and astrology, love, sensual pleasure, and friendship).

The *human qualities* form, in the infinite spaces, societies, fraternities, or separate nations, and just as it is impossible for us to devote ourselves, at the same time, to the study of all the "sciences" taught in the universities, it is impossible for us to put ourselves in contact, at one time, with all the hierarchies presiding, as we have said, over human qualities and faculties.

Consequently, to enter into communication with these hierarchies it is necessary first of all to determine with just which of them we wish to join ourselves.

In addition, it is necessary to know the particular laws that obtain there and emanate from there; and it is necessary to know the name of the fraternity to which this hierarchy belongs.

It is not permitted to reveal to the profane the law of each hierarchy, but everyone has the possibility of discovering the correspondence in the human "science" that reflects it.

Attach yourself, therefore, to the study of the various disciplines enumerated above, and strive to penetrate the spirit of their laws. This is the lower path, which leads to the higher path.

Regarding the names of the hierarchies and of the interplanetary societies or fraternities, you will find some of them in the official religions. But if you don't even do this research, you will know the *names* when you shall have penetrated the *essences*. It would not be of any use to you to know them sooner.

When, in the course of the exercise of tirauclairism, you shall have succeeded in uniting yourself with one of the interplanetary hierarchies, the *influence* that you receive from it will stay with you for some time, and that will prevent you from uniting right away with another hierarchy whose laws are different.

This is why it will be necessary to wait, according to the case, from three to seven months, before trying again.

To align yourself with a person who is absent, turn in the direction of the geographic point where that person is, and reconstruct in your imagination his or her physiognomy and the atmosphere that surrounds that person.

If you methodically act accordingly, every night, at the same time, you will feel, little by little, that the image evoked takes on life within you.

Soon, it will be in you, at your first call, as a presence that will at the same time penetrate and envelop you.

You will feel its influence and warmth, and you will be able to suggest to it whatever you wish: an idea or a feeling.

But continue to persevere, until the person you have imagined in the tirauclairism exercise becomes detached from you and appears before you, at first transparent, and then, little by little, living and *as if* in flesh and bone.

If you succeed in that, a solid link will be created between you and the person who interests you, and, if you wish, you will get their collaboration within the sphere that you choose.

If you are an artisan of the Great Work, if you participate in the reconstruction of the visible and invisible world, according to the law of the Great Master, you will not wish for alignment with another human being except for a purpose useful to the sacred task.

In this case the higher entities will come to your aid more easily, and they will favor your occult liaison with the desired collaborator. They will help you to infuse into him or her the qualities that they do not have, to open before them horizons of which they are unaware, to give them the courage and energy that they are lacking.

At the same time, do not be surprised if they experience the gifts, which you give them from yourself or attract to them from the corresponding hierarchies, as personal revelations, and, above all, don't fret if, instead of the recognition and love that you would like, they show you disgust or even hatred. It is the entities, to whom they were submitted, who thus take revenge, because your gifts trouble and vex them.

But have patience and send thoughts charged with love to the one whom you have chosen, so that your good sentiments may act as beneficial rain, which makes seeds sprout and plants come up for the glory of God.

You will later harvest your share of joy.

If you wish to enter into alignment with an absent person for a personal or egotistical reason, one for which, consequently, the higher forces are slow to come to your aid—for you distract them thus from their habitual occupations—you will need greater and longer patience to obtain the desired result.

Still, with perseverance you will succeed even so, for Man can master and dominate interplanetary forces, even when his purposes are unworthy.

This is the serious responsibility of the human being and the reason that guided initiates when they wrapped their special knowledge in a thick veil of mystery.

If today we reveal the secrets, it is because the hour of Light is near. The force, which must win out, is near to us.

PART III

magic

9

ASTROLOGY, PERFUMES, COLORS, SOUNDS

I n the preceding chapters we have indicated the mental exercises to which the student must, in the beginning, devote himself if he wishes that the rest of our teaching should truly be profitable to him on the upward path of achieving individual perfection.

We have said that it is necessary to learn *volantia,* that is to say, to acquire the capacity to calmly send out a mental force to its chosen goal.

From this principle, generally symbolized by the letter A, one passes to *decretism;* that is to say, one develops within oneself the capacity to emanate peremptory orders, calmly and surely, without the least doubt about obtaining the desired effect.

One passes then to the sign S, which symbolizes *posism,* that is to say, the combination of rules concerning the body and the spirit, which permits the creation of forms and states, whose symbolism one recovers in Freemasonry under the signs V and O.

One devotes oneself, finally, to *tirauclairism,* or to the evocation of the forms of living beings and immaterial essences, symbolized by the Names.

If the student has acquired sufficient ability in the preliminary exercises, he should be able to accomplish all of his projects.

But he should be on guard against various and innumerable emotions that will assail him when the influence that he emanates is at its strongest.

It is nature that defends itself thus against those who attempt to free themselves from it.

Do not become discouraged, you who are opening the door of the temple of infinite Wisdom! The man who knows how to make use of his means triumphs over Nature.

ASTROLOGY

In Astrology, as in Sexual Magic, the moon, this second principal planet of our system, is certainly the most important factor.

It is necessary, therefore, to bear this in mind:

1. The moon, feminine planet, favors feminine power.
2. When the moon is in its waxing phase, its feminine form increases proportionally. This is the propitious period for the woman's magical actions, for the lunar vibratory currents are then favorable to her. For the man, this period is good for passive operations of reception, as well as for the correction of his acquired or developed faculties.
3. When the moon wanes, the period is propitious for the active operations of the man, for the projection of influence upon another, to command, to modify the "volt" (magical figurine

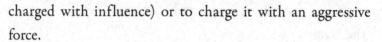

charged with influence) or to charge it with an aggressive force.

4. The variations of the moon's magnetic current are at their maximum between the twenty-eighth day and the first day of the lunar cycle. They are at their minimum, which is negative or feminine, between the fourteenth and fifteenth days of this cycle.

5. During the masculine period of the lunar month, one can operate actively, also benefiting from the influence of the masculine planets. During the feminine periods—second and third quarters—one should devote oneself to passive actions.

To determine a person's force potential, according to their individual horoscope, one should algebraically add the strengths and weaknesses of the planets that are found in the birth chart.

In this way one obtains, for each of the seven planets of our system, a number indicating the strength of its influence upon the person in question.

This number can be advantageously employed for the preparation of the particular perfume, color, and melody that are very helpful for the realization of personal goals, as well as for magical operations with a more extended range.

COLORS

To find a person's individual color, the color that synthesizes a time, or the color that favors the execution of a particular magical operation, one should first proceed to the study of the astrological relationships of all the planetary forces, in accordance with table 9.1.

Table 9.1. Table of Planetary Correspondences

Planet and Sound	Metal	Number	Color	Perfume		Stone
☀ C = do	gold	6	yellow	orange (peel) marsh mallow (leaf) violet of Parma lavender	= 400 gr. = 100 gr. = 300 gr. = 200 gr.	diamond
☽ F = fa	silver	9	silvery white	saffron linden (flower) tumain [thyme?] goat leaf (leaf)	= 300 gr. = 200 gr. = 300 gr. = 200 gr.	pearl
☿ E = mi	quick-silver (mercury)	8	multi-colored	anise datura stramonium apple (juice) acacia (bark) garlic planetary perfume	= 200 gr. = 400 gr. = 250 gr. = 100 gr. = 50 gr. = 167 gr.	sardonyx
♀ A = la	copper	7	green	pineapple (juice) lily (leaf) lilac (leaf) rose (leaf) myrtle (leaf) mandrake (leaf)	= 320 gr. = 100 gr. = 150 gr. = 135 gr. = 245 gr. = 50 gr.	emerald
♂ G = sol	iron	5	red	Aaron [arum lily?] (whole plant) mint hemp (leaf) lilac (leaf) garlic (whole plant)	= 215 gr. = 335 gr. = 150 gr. = 120 gr. = 180 gr.	ruby
♃ B = ti	tin	4	blue	violet (flower) sesame (seed) aloe (fruit) goat leaf (stem)	= 280 gr. = 250 gr. = 150 gr. = 320 gr.	amethyst
♄ D = re	lead	3	black	hyoscamus niger [black henbane] tobacco (root) mandrake (root) broad bean cumin (seed) opium	= 250 gr. = 150 gr. = 380 gr. = 20 gr. = 50 gr. = 50 gr.	onyx

1. For each of the planets of the horoscope, suitably established, one should determine the strengths (+) and the weaknesses (-).

2. One should add the positive values (+) and the negative values (-), and from that one should establish the balance, or definitive sum, for each planet, separately.

3. One should prepare a disk with a diameter of two feet, and then divide the circumference into as many equal parts as there are units in the sum total of the balances found for each planet.

4. One should divide the disk into as many equal sectors.

5. For each of the planets, take the number of sectors that is equal to the number of its balance, established according to table 9.1. Balances that are less than zero, or negative, will obviously need to be rejected.

6. Mercury's sector should be further divided into as many equal parts as there are planets taken into consideration, not counting itself.

7. The sector for each color should be painted with its characteristic color. One should repeat these same colors, and in the same order, in the subdivisions of Mercury's sector.

8. One should fix the disk, thus prepared, on a rotating axis, and make it turn rapidly, in such a way as to obtain the illusion of a single color. This color will be the one that was to be found.

9. One should make a faithful copy of it.

Example

Let us suppose that, after having established a birth chart and consulted table 9.1, we have the following results:

Table 9.2

Planets	☀	☽	☿	♀	♂	♃	♄	
Strengths	30	50	45	45	45	35	25	
Weaknesses	10	43	5	3	15	15	35	
Totals	20	7	40	42	30	20	−10	End result = 159

We then divide our disk into 159 equal sectors, and, in conformity to the balances found, we take, respectively:

Table 9.3

20 sectors for ☀

7 sectors for ☽

40 sectors for ☿

42 sectors for ♀

30 sectors for ♂

20 sectors for ♃

Saturn has no place on the disk, because its balance is negative.

The sectors of the different planets being drawn, we give them colors as follows:

Table 9.4

☀ in yellow

☽ in white

♀ in green

♂ in red

♃ in blue

The sector for Mercury, subdivided into five small and equal sectors, will receive all the colors: yellow, white, green, red, and blue, as shown in figure 9.1.

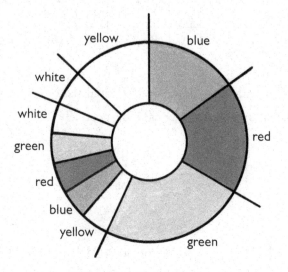

Fig. 9.1. Natal Chart

The study of the influence of colors leads us to results that are as surprising as they are strange. No magical recipe could be efficaciously established without the factor of one's individual color, obtained according to the method that we have just explained.

PERFUMES

In table 9.1 one finds the corresponding flowers and plants for the seven planets, which especially absorb their qualities.

To prepare an individual perfume, one should therefore choose the necessary plants, according to the table and according to the horoscope of the person involved, and one should make *force extracts* from them.

These can be obtained neither by distillation nor by means of pressing, but only by macerating them in hot pork grease.

This should be done as follows:

1. One puts the grease into pure water, which is then brought to a boil three times.
2. Add some course cooking salt (sea salt does not have the same properties), in the proportion of two units by weight of salt to one unit of grease.
3. Leave the grease, well mixed with the salt, in a bath of cold running water, or under the tap, until all the salt is gone.
4. Heat the grease again, and macerate the plants in it.
5. Immediately separate the macerated plants from the grease, and allow them to cool.
6. Cut them, when they are cold, into small cubes, which should be macerated again for all of fourteen days in alcohol obtained from the distillation of a good white wine.

To proportion the plant extracts obtained in this way, with a view to the preparation of an individual perfume, one should have recourse to the method cited above for the colors.

Using the sample data given above, one would have:

Table 9.5

☀ 20 parts	☿ 40/5 of ☀
☽ 7 parts	☿ 40/5 of ☽
♀ 42 parts	☿ 40/5 of ♀
♂ 30 parts	☿ 40/5 of ♂
♃ 20 parts	☿ 40/5 of ♃

A person's individual color, obtained by the method that we teach, optically expresses the synthesis of their character.

We have said that one can also obtain the characteristic color of a mental state. For that it is necessary to establish the proportional value of the occult forces that focus and attract the influences that are necessary for the effect.

The same horoscopic procedure will help us to do that. When we have found the desired color, we shall surround ourselves with it for the magical operation, in the form of lighting and painted decorations.

We shall do the same thing for the perfume, which must reinforce the benefic effect of the color.

For an individual perfume that is for a woman, it is necessary to add a mixture of essences extracted from the flower of *Chenopodium vulveria* in the ratio of two grams of *Chenopodium* to ten grams of prepared mixture.

For a man's perfume, one should use *Kastania sauerdon* in the same proportions.

Individual perfumes, prepared according to our methods, are very efficacious for the exercise of posism.

One should also make use of them, in combination with the influence of colors, to charge the "volt," or any other material, with the force favorable to an occult bond with a living person, an entity, or a spiritual hierarchy.

SOUNDS AND THE COMPOSITION
OF PERSONAL MELODIES

Table 9.1 gives us, for each planetary force, the corresponding sound, which it evokes by analogy of vibrations.

In the magical recipes that we give in this book, we don't concern ourselves too much with effects obtained by music, for the other effects that we have cited, and of which we shall offer further citations, are sufficiently effective for the realization of splendid phenomena.

Still, to obtain effects that are extraordinary and surpassing all the others in their marvelousness, it is necessary to accept the challenge of the acoustical experience, which is also found to be at the base of the *intonations* of all rites of evocation.

It is necessary to note and to remember that, without the correct pitch, words of power, such as *mantras* and others, do not have all their power.

The main principles that can be extracted from the occult science of sounds come down to this:

1. Abbreviate the numbers indicating the respective strength of each planet in such a way that the maximum can be expressed by 5 and the minimum by 1, with a precision of 0.5. Reject negative values and 0. You will thus have:

Table 9.6

☉	☽	☿	♀	♂	♃	♄
20	7	40	42	30	20	0
3	1	5	5	4	3	0

2. Form the scale of strengths, as follows:

Table 9.7

♀	☿	♂	♃	☀	☽
5	5	4	3	3	1

3. Write the strengths on the musical staff, the design of which
   is shown on page 51 (fig. 9.2).
   a) according to paragraph 2 (fig. 9.2)
   b) according to the numbers symbolizing the planets (fig. 3)
   c) a scale of natural strength (fig. 4)
   d) Put in the strength that characterizes the intended goal
      (in our example, Venus), and place these representations
      in the following order: a, b; b, a; d and d reversed (fig. 5).
   e) In the diagram cited, each planetary force has its relative
      value, according to a scale from 1 to 5: 1/16; 1/8; 1/4; 1/2;
      1/1.

In translating these values into the corresponding musical notes,
one will need to accentuate the most important influences by rein-
forcing the sound, whether it be by multiplication of the strings or
pipes of the instrument, or by prolonging the note.

The musical octave may be chosen at will, for the correspondence of the note with the planetary force does not depend upon
its tone. The *do* or the *la,* whether flat or sharp, has the same
efficacy.

The tolerance of 0.5 allows one to replace the second with a
half-tone if needed. Therefore you can raise your note with a sharp

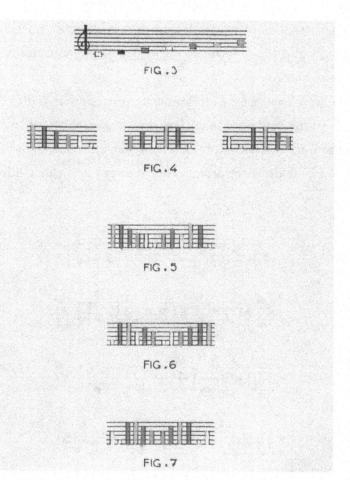

Figure 9.2

or lower it with a flat without modifying the magical influence.

While following all these rules, one will have no trouble dividing the series of written notes into a suitable number of measures.

The melody obtained should be put into an automatic music box (today we would use a phonograph), which one will play during the operation. In this way the combined effect of color and perfume will be reinforced by the melody.

The syllables of human languages, as they relate to the musical notes, as also the modulations of different pronunciations, form a separate science.

This science helps us to formulate ritual prayers and to discover the treasures contained in ancient rites. But, in this book, we cannot occupy ourselves with it, for it would take us far afield.

We only draw the attention of the reader to this truth, which

Fig. 9.3. Magical Melody

confirms our conviction that by seriously delving into all the laws of nature, one can achieve excellent results for ascent on the path of individual and collective improvement.

"All that is below is like that which is above." Look at and study that which is around you, and you will know how to climb.

10

MAGICAL SEXUAL OPERATIONS

GENERAL RULES

In the foregoing the reader has been able to study the rules and principles that permit, if they are applied correctly, the accomplishment of tremendous things.

We shall now go on to the sexual operations themselves, which could not have their full effectiveness without all that has been explained up to this point.

These operations are the basis of the mysteries known by the name of *Mahi Kaligua,** which derive from the *eulidic* principle, of which we have spoken at the beginning of this work.

One can practice them for very diverse goals, but we shall limit ourselves to seven principal ones.

---

*[In extant works of Randolph this is usually spelled as "Mahi-caligna." The confusion of "n" and "u" suggests that Naglowska was, indeed, working from a handwritten manuscript. —*Trans.*]

1. The charging of the "volts" and other fluid condensers.
2. The regeneration of strength and vital energy and the reinforcement of magnetic power.
3. The production of magnetic influence, with a view to the submission of the man to the woman, or of the woman to the man.
4. The refinement of power or of the senses in general.
5. The determination, at will, of the sex of the infant to be conceived, or the reinforcement of its cerebral or corporal capacities, in general.
6. The provocation of superhuman, spiritual, and sublime visions.
7. The realization of a particular project or desire of the operator, in any idea category.*[1]

Assuming that the student has studied and well understood all that we have explained in the preceding chapters, we give, here below, the sixteen† principal rules that he must follow, in addition, to devote himself without danger to the special exercises of sexual magic.

1. Sexual union is to be thought of as a prayer.
   The man who lives with his woman in perfect harmony

---

*[This list, which appears on page 75 of the French edition of *Magia Sexualis,* is a paraphrase and slight reordering of a list in the *Mysteries of Eulis,* which is probably its source. It appears (as the "Ansairetic Arcanum") in the Hermetic Brotherhood of Luxor publication, *The Mysteries of Eros.* It is also related to a similar list, called "The Glories of Eulis" in Aleister Crowley's IX degree instruction in his *Liber Agape.* None of the other lists, though, include the first item of the Randolph/Naglowska list, concerning the charging of "volts" and other fluid condensers. —*Trans.*]
†Naglowska's original text said "twenty."

will understand us easily, and he who has had the good fortune to embrace a woman loved and loving, in all purity of sentiment and intention, will recall that in no other circumstance of life did he plunge so deeply to launch himself so vigorously toward God and Perfection as in that radiant moment when all his conjoined forces touched the root of the opposite sex.

For when the sexual act is perfect, the union of the man with the woman is accomplished in all the spheres of their respective beings, and their forces are then increased tenfold on high as they are here below. The prayer, *this* prayer, is always heard.

But it is necessary that the petition, the wish, the *object* of the prayer be formulated and imagined clearly.

If the man and the woman imagine the same objective, or wish for the same thing, that is better; but the prayer of one of the two is also effective, for it carries with it, in the amorous spasm, the creative power of the other.

2. Do not mix precious metal with base matter: unite yourself with a woman of high morals.

   Do not take, for the magical operation, either a prostitute, or an inexperienced virgin, or a minor under the age of eighteen years, or another's wife; but accomplish the solemn act with your wife or with your lover.

   It is necessary, in any case, that the woman chosen for the rite should already have experience with a man and should still be capable of energy, of will, of affection and deep emotion; for the climax of both is necessary in order that your prayer should be effective. It is also necessary that the *exudive** moment of the woman should coincide with the *expulsive* one of the man, for only thus is magic accomplished.

3. The union of the man with the woman must be innocent.

Voluptuousness and pleasure must not be the principal goal of the union.

Beyond carnal pleasure, aim for a union of souls, if you want your prayer to be heard.

If you conform yourself to these principles, for you the sexual act will be a source of spiritual and bodily strength and a cause of health, joyfulness, and peace. You will thus find that which, in magic, is called "the soul's fortune."

4. The bodies must be clean.

Hygiene is always a sacred duty, but above all when you prepare yourself for the rite of sexual union.

We shall tell you further on that certain *preparations* last seven days and forty-one days. Cleanliness will then be particularly strict.

5. Keep your intentions secret.

Silence concentrates your strength and multiplies it. That is why, when you have entered into the preparatory period of the magical act, do not frequent society overly, and speak as little as possible.

6. Formulate your desire in advance and do not forget it at the moment of coitus, during which it will be necessary for you to remain silent.

---

*[The form "exudive" is one of Randolph's marvelous neologisms. The standard form is "exudative." I've kept Randolph's form, as Naglowska did, because I like it—and also because it is representative of his characteristic vocabulary. This whole section is paraphrased from *The Mysteries of Eulis.* —*Trans.*]

7. Before, during, and after the act of love, keep within you a clear image of that for which you wish.

   The exercises of volantia, posism, and decretism will be a great help to you during the period of preparation.

8. Nourish yourself simply, and prefer natural foods; do not take too much; don't take in too many liquids; avoid grease, alcohol, and spices.

   Sleep on a hard bed, with your head to the north, with flat pillows.

   Your bedroom should be cool and well ventilated.

9. Take an air bath two times per week.

   Breathe, then, deeply, and keep the air in your lungs as long as possible. Know that each additional minute that you can hold it adds ten days to your life.

10. Do not see your woman too often, and only when both of you are well in the mood.

    Sleep in separate bedrooms, and do not have sexual union more than one or two times per week.

    The man should never touch a woman who is not excited, and he must not leave her before both orgasms have passed.

    This is one of the most important recommendations.

11. Do not take the woman if you are angry or if you have been drinking.

12. Go to bed at an early hour, and, when you are falling asleep, trust in yourself and in the force of the higher laws.

13. Do not forget this important axiom: love is the root of life.

    From love is born, according to the circumstances, passions, transports, impulses, good or bad, the divine or human flame, demons or gods.

May your love unite you with God!

14. The instant when the seed of the man passes into the body of the woman, who accepts it, is the most fertile moment, the most powerful, the most moving of human life.

If he is, then, under the influence of carnal passion, of bestial instinct, the man is killing himself, he is lost, he becomes demoralized.

To the woman, he brings sickness and psychic and bodily disorganization.

If a child is conceived, he breeds an assassin, a mental cripple, a miserable being.

If, on the other hand, the union of the man with the woman is effected in the harmony of reciprocal love, and if, consequently, the occult forces, spread throughout the surrounding environment, participate with joy in the solemn act, then the man and the woman find themselves regenerated therefrom and the fruit of their embrace is blessed.

The child of love is a child of the higher forces, and the prayer of two hearts united is an efficacious prayer.

15. If a man ardently wishes for a force or power, and keeps that wish from the moment when he penetrates the woman until the moment when he leaves her, his wish is necessarily fulfilled.

The hell that reigns in households at present is due above all to the bad habit the man has acquired of withdrawing before ejaculation, because he no longer wishes to procreate.

Because of that, hell is installed at the root of the two

beings, for they are prostituting love, while ignoring the Great Reason, the primordial *why* of life.

The seed that is lost and not converted causes degeneration.

16. All forces and powers emanate from the femininity of God, from which also issue all impulses.*

Draw out the divine force that is in complete love, in real fellow-feeling, in the emotion that gives you beauty.

The brain is sterile, and its strength is rapidly used up; that is why we, the *Eulidians,* look for spiritual triumph not in the intellect, which becomes fatigued and does not succeed, but in love's will, endlessly fertile.

When one among us, having the healing gift, undertakes a healing, he does not call on the intellect, but on love.

His face becomes sweet and kind, his hands become caressing, his heart wishes and speaks, and a good result is infallibly obtained.

For love, fellow-feeling, kindness, form a ladder, which rises toward *innumerable* forces, the power and wisdom of the Heavens.†

THE FIVE PRINCIPAL POSITIONS

The following drawings represent schematically the five principal positions that the couple must take in the course of the sexual magic operation for the *prayer of love.*

These five positions, which rule the mental current, favor, respectively, the following effects.

---

*[Per Randolph, "from the SHE side of God." —*Trans.*]

†[At this point we reach the end of *The Mysteries of Eulis* and Naglowska's paraphrase of it. Randolph only adds that we should study *Seership!* along with it. —*Trans.*]

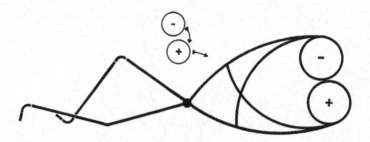

Fig. 10.1. Position 1

Fig. 10.2. Position 2

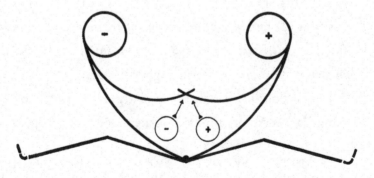

Fig. 10.3. Position 3

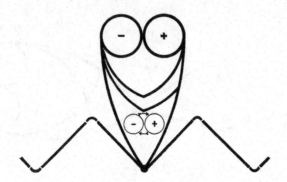

Fig. 10.4. Position 4

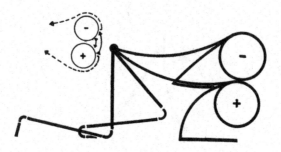

Fig. 10.5. Position 5

1. Position (1) corrects the senses and the capacities of the operators, in the case where they themselves are the object of their influence.

2. Position (2) favors the projection of influence to the exterior (*we call that: the exterior circle*): upon one or several chosen persons, or upon the higher spheres.

   It is propitious, further, for charging a "volt," for creating larvae,*[2] or for any other aggressive operation

---

*[The "larva" is a poorly defined entity that inhabits the spaces between the spheres and can be engendered through certain sexual operations. Both Randolph and Blavatsky made use of this concept. Randolph gives an early use of the term in his book *The Unveiling* (1860), when quoting Thomas Lake Harris. —*Trans.*]

against a person, whether they are aware of it or not.

3. Position (3) produces the same effects as position (2), but it also serves to receive or orient the force of the exterior circle.

   This position cannot be realized unless the man and the woman are in agreement.

4. Position (4) is effective for harmonizing—as two instruments that must play the same music—the man and the woman devoting themselves to the magical operation of love.

   It harmonizes the difference that separates their respective natures and condenses the feeling.

   In this position, the man and the woman must operate with one common accord.

5. Position (5) permits the man to influence the woman without her being aware of it.

   Also, when the two operants taking this position are in agreement, it serves to project a vigorous influence into the exterior circle.

These five positions are constructed in conformity to the normal law of opening of the aura.

The schematic drawings reproduced here assume that the active operator is the man; but it may also be otherwise, for it is not said that the woman cannot assume the initiative in the magical operation.

If the woman is the one who directs the operation, one should transpose our drawings according to the law of natural analogies.

II

CORRECTION OF THE SENSES AND FACULTIES

We now come to the problem of practical exploitation of the magical sexual force.

We repeat again that this exploitation cannot be useful or profitable to the student who has not first studied, seriously and patiently, the manner of working with the mental forces that one develops in exercising decretism, volantia, posism, and tirauclairism, expounded in the preceding chapters of this book.

For, to exploit a force, it is necessary to know how to master it. Let this be understood also for the rest of our teachings.

We have already said that, before beginning the magical operation as such, it is necessary to go through a period of preparation, divided into two phases: the first of seven days, and the second of forty-one days.

In order that everything should go as desired, conform yourself to the following prescriptions.

1. Choose a peaceful room for the experimental work, where no sound comes in from the street.

   Put shutters or thick curtains over the windows to shield you from the daylight, and wait until the room temperature remains between 78 degrees and 68 degrees Fahrenheit.

   During all the period of your experiments, do not allow anyone to enter the room.

2. Carefully prepare the perfume, corresponding to the planetary force that you propose to attract, as well as the color, which you will distribute through the room by means of lighting or decor.

3. The first phase of the preparatory period, which lasts seven days, must begin on the first day of the moon's third quarter.

4. During these seven days the woman, chosen for her magical experience, must not come into the room.

5. Fix with precision the hour at which you will operate.

   It is at this hour that you will do your preparatory exercises every day, during the period of seven days, and during that of forty-one days, which will follow immediately after the first.

6. During the period of seven days, do the posism exercises, which will attract to you the faculty that you wish for.

   Study well the gesture that characterizes this faculty.

   Spread the necessary perfume throughout the room, but do not perfume yourself and do not put any perfume on your clothes.

   Spread the desired color throughout the room by means of lighting.

7. When, by the exercise of posism, you shall have firmly established the desired faculty as part of your mental state, begin to combine the posism exercise with that of tirauclairism.

8. During the seven days of the first phase of the preparation, do not work more than a half-hour per day.

9. On the eighth day you will begin the second phase of the preparation, which will last, as we've said, for forty-one days.

   On that day, perfume not only the room but also your palms and your solar plexus.

   Do not forget, then, to add *Kastania* essence to the perfume.

   Bring in the woman.

10. Illuminate the room with the color chosen, and have your companion lie on her back.

    Arouse her. Speak as little as possible.

11. At the opportune moment, accomplish the act of union, using position number 1: the front of the man touching the front of the woman.

12. By means of decretism, volantia, and posism, accentuate your desire at the instant of ejaculation, and energetically think of the thing wished for before, during, and after the act.

13. Once the *magical prayer* is finished, send the woman back out. She must leave without saying a word.

14. You will repeat the operation together every three days, for the whole period of forty-one days.

15. During the two interval days, the man will continue his work, as during the seven-day phase, and always at the same hour.

16. After the period of forty-one days, if everything has been done correctly, the faculty, sense, or force that you have wished for will have been acquired in your mental makeup.

　　If, in a special circumstance, you wish to accentuate this force, or this faculty, or this sense, breathe the perfume used during the operation.

The rite of magical love, of which we have expounded the laws and the methods, may be accomplished for purposes as diverse as life itself, but never forget that the law of polarizations, and that of reflection, cast back upon the operator the good and the ill that he causes others.

　　Thus it is that the crime implies the punishment, from the beginning.

　　If you operate in working position number 5, while using your individual perfume, with a view to suggesting love and voluptuous pleasure to your woman, you will be able to keep her under your influence for as long as you like.

　　The force, whose key you have here, can also be used to ameliorate or modify the circulation of the blood, as you wish. This allows you to work psychic and physical healings.

THE SEX OF THE
CHILD

In the chapter dealing with the polarization of the sexes, we have formulated the law that raises the veil of Isis, behind which is hidden the fundamental mystery of everything that is born and develops in the universe.

All the rites of the secret societies and the mystical fraternities, as well as certain "mysteries" of the official religions, take inspiration from this primordial law and its derivatives, which explain to us how the mental current, produced during the ecstasy of coitus, is formed and oriented.

Under normal conditions, which is to say, when nature is left to itself, a single goal is pursued in the act of love: the creation of a new individual, by means of the conjunction of opposite sexual forces.

This end, this insatiable will of nature to create something new, is complicated by the no less peremptory law, which is itself also a will, of repetition of the preceding patterns. This law is called "atavism," and it completes the law of polarization of the sexes, which we have formulated above, in the following manner.

At the instant of coitus, the woman creates, in her mental sphere, the image of a man, while the man creates the image of a woman. According to the current that carries it, the child will be male or female.

According to this law, it would suffice, for predicting the sex of the newborn, to establish with exactitude which of the two—the father or the mother—has stronger imaginative power; and one would weaken, by physical fatigue, which would also be reflected mentally, the woman or the man, according as a daughter or a son should be wished.

Still, practically, the thing is not so simple, for the imaginative power of an individual varies, and it is difficult to foresee its quality at a moment fixed in advance.

That is why we counsel the couple who wish the birth of a boy or a girl to have recourse, there also, to the magical sexual operation, conforming themselves to the following rules.

1. To produce a boy:

   Perfume the room with the perfume of Mars, to which one has added the essence of *Kastania,* in the ratio 1:1.3.

   Operate in red light.

   To produce a girl: Use the perfume of Venus with the essence of *Chenopodium,* mixed in the ratio 1:1.

   Illuminate the room with green light.

2. The prayer of love—which may be formulated by the man or the woman individually, or by the two spouses by a common agreement—will be of considerable effectiveness.

   If the prayer is only made by one of the spouses, take position number 1. If you will pray together, choose position number 4.

3. During the period of psychic preparation—which will last seven days—it is helpful to make use of a picture, representing a man or a woman, depending upon whether one wishes to give birth to a boy or a girl.

The seven-day preparation suffices. One should operate on the eighth day.

If one conforms oneself strictly to these rules, the desired result will be infallibly obtained.

But it is necessary that the father and the mother should be normal.

13

ϝLUID CONDENSERS

These notes are written for the students of our fraternity.

They should serve them as directives for a real initiation into the path of Truth.

We believe that it is useless to lose oneself in the theoretical considerations that fill so many works by ancient and modern occultists.

The theories, the theses, the philosophical opinions, rarely provide sufficient light, and they never give the incontestable scientific proofs without which truth cannot triumph.

Our method is to place the student, right in the beginning, in front of some undeniable experimental facts.

The student who has some intelligence and some goodwill shall decide for himself, from what he has seen and touched, theories like ours, and if he perseveres, if he does not abandon the initiatic voyage begun, because of his difficulties and the numerous privations that it implies, the good student will come to know, little by little, by himself, the true doctrine of wisdom.

He will then be its faithful adept.

Meanwhile, to make the path easier, to sweeten the rough spots on the way a little for all those who would like to follow us, we summarize here the results of our personal labors.

As one knows, we have consecrated long years to the experimental verification of all that we have been able to discover, in the form of counsels and practices, in the ancient and modern works.

In this way we have been able to proceed to a meticulous triage, to separate the true from the false, the positive from the illusory, and we have thus acquired the right to affirm that what we advise and teach is in conformity with pure scientific truth.

The keys, which we reveal, are sufficient to allow each one to do his own experiment.

The general ideas that we advance can be verified by anyone, and there is no need for anything more than a little courage and goodwill for taking the first step.

The joy that always crowns conscientious effort will sustain the seeker's strength on the most arid paths.

Magic is a science.

It is the only science that really, theoretically and practically, concerns itself with the still-hidden, higher forces of Nature.

It declares and proves that the universe, in its totality, as in each of its tiniest bits, is subject to particular fluid influences, which official science can know exactly and which it will be able to discover on the day when it wishes, which are the basis of every psychic or physical phenomenon.

To work with these forces, according to the laws that govern them, it is necessary, first of all, to concentrate them into a point or upon a given surface.

One may, after that, orient them and channel them at will.

These operations, which are very important and which offer very diverse possibilities for realization, can be done in four different ways.

1. The operator can make use of his own energy.
2. He can act with the exterior forces, by means of induction and correspondences.
3. He can bind the exterior forces to any individual chosen for the purpose.
4. He can bind the forces to an object or, in general, to a matter of his choice.

This last procedure has been known, for thousands of years, in talismanic magic. It is also useful for what is known as the *charging of the "volts,"* of which we have spoken in a preceding chapter.

At the same time, in verifying the technique for these preparations, as they have been practiced up to the present, we ascertained that a lack of laboratory experience often led, for condensation of fluids, to the utilization of insufficiently pure materials. In this manner, quite often, materials chosen for making a condenser were only partially suitable, which, obviously, diminished accordingly the effectiveness of the talismans and the "volts."

To avoid this error and to obtain henceforth results that are perfect, we have studied and prepared three types of irreproachable fluid condensers—two liquid and one solid—which, in our experience, have shown themselves to be completely satisfactory.

The first of these three types of condenser is employed by us in the form of layers or coatings that we gradually extend over objects to which we wish to attach talismanic virtues.

The second, which we keep in special vials, serves us for the preparation of very effective liquid drugs.

The third type, the solid fluid condenser, is employed in our laboratories for the fabrication of "volts."

Here is the proportional table for the preparation of our drugs.

Liquid Condenser for Coatings

White wine	120 grams
Juice of lily leaves	4 grams
Juice of mandrake	18 grams
Juice of chamomile	19 grams
Juice of poplar leaves	48 grams
Poplar charcoal	15 grams
Extract of lily flower	2 grams
Extract of mandrake	3 grams
Extract of chamomile	1 gram
Extract of poplar	4 grams
Milk sugar	50 grams
Lactucarium	25 grams
Liquid gold	6 grams
Gelatin	80 grams
Copal oil	25 grams

Liquid Condenser for Bottling

Juice of lily leaves	1 gram
Juice of mandrake leaves	8 grams
Juice of chamomile leaves	9 grams
Juice of poplar leaves	20 grams
Extract of lily flower	3 grams
Extract of mandrake	13 grams
Extract of chamomile	5 grams
Extract of poplar	32 grams
Milk sugar	60 grams
Lactucarium	36 grams

Solid Condenser

Mandrake charcoal	80 grams
Iron	20 grams
Bronze powder	15 grams
Milk sugar	40 grams
Gold	18 grams
Lactucarium	80 grams
Poplar charcoal	16 grams
Beeswax	16 grams

For these drugs to function as desired, it is necessary, in their preparation, to conform oneself to the following recommendations.

1. The plant extracts must be prepared by maceration in pure alcohol, where it is necessary to leave them for fourteen whole days.

   The glass being used for this operation must not be exposed to the sun or, in general, to daylight.

   The temperature of the room where the glass with alcohol used for the maceration of the extracts is kept must be maintained constantly at 90 degrees Fahrenheit.

   For every 100 grams of herbs, 120 grams of alcohol are necessary.
2. The pressed extracts are prepared by compilation.
3. To obtain plant charcoals, seal the plant hermetically in a ball of blown glass, which you will immediately plunge into the flame of a wood or coal fire.
4. The beeswax, which we recommend for certain mixtures, must first be boiled three times in pure water.

5. The glazed gum that is used must be washed in cold, running water, as also the copal oil.

6. Before proceeding to the mixing of the characteristic compositions, one should take care to hermetically seal, in a glass or a vial, a sufficient volume of fluid condenser.

   This glass or vial, containing the condenser, must remain in cold, running water for ten whole days.

7. When one dries the plants that will be used for the magical preparations, one should watch carefully lest they come under the influence of daylight. One should take care, further, to keep the laboratory at 90 degrees Fahrenheit maximum.

8. To isolate the fluid condensers from daylight, one should wrap the glass or the vial that contains it with several layers of a natural silk fabric, which one should wash carefully in running water before using.

   The operation of mixing several condensers must be done by artificial light.

14

"VOLTS"

All experimental magic is based on the laws of correspondences, of sympathies, and of polarizations.

While the laws of polarization determine the force of attraction between two opposite poles (+ and −), the laws of correspondence and sympathy require that all etheric forces distributed through space should have, on Earth, their corresponding elements or materials, as well as their sound, their color, their rhythm, and their sympathizing perfume.

An in-depth study of these various correspondences allows us to operate successfully with the aid of solid fluid condensers (type 3), which we call "volts."

These condensers are figurines prepared in a special manner (see below) and which one charges, according to the method that we indicate here, with the psychic force of an individual in order to influence them, for good or ill, with the help of the laws of correspondences and sympathies; it may be to cure them of a sickness, or it may be to correct or improve their nature, or it may be, lastly, to cast good or ill fortune upon them.

The preparation of a "volt" requires the following operations.

1. The defining and fabrication of the subject's individual perfume and color.

2. The introduction into the solid condenser of the liquid condenser number 2 (see above), in the ratio of 20:1; and the introduction of the individual perfume, in the ratio of 10:1.

3. The shaping of the material, thus prepared, into a statuette, reproducing with maximum resemblance the entire silhouette, or the part of the subject's body that is to be influenced.

4. The mixing into the fluid condenser number 1 (see above), of a color in powder, so as to obtain the individual color desired.

5. Painting the statuette with the color thus obtained. Two coats, and often three, of such paint are required.

6. Washing the statuette, when the paint is quite dry, in very clean running water.

7. The vessel, into which the statuette will immediately be introduced for its isolation, must be prepared in the following manner.

    It should be selected of thick and pure glass, and one should cover it, inside and out, with four layers of natural silk fabric, well washed beforehand.

    The exterior surface of the vessel should also receive, before the layers of silk, a light layer of an amalgam of gold and mercury.

    One should treat the lid of the vessel in the same manner.

    When the statuette has been introduced into the vessel, which one will then seal hermetically with the lid, one should put the vessel with the statuette into a hardwood box.

8. To charge the "volt" with the energy of the subject for whom it is destined, it suffices for the latter to keep it in his bedroom, or, better still, in his pocket, for ten whole days.

After that, the subject in question must put the statuette back into the vessel himself, and the vessel into the box; and it is essential that no one should assist in this operation and, above all, that no one except the subject should touch the statuette at that time.

One may easily imagine that any stranger who should mix his curiosity into this operation would be charging the "volt" with a contrary influence, which could also be dangerous.

For that reason, do not break this rule of privacy, if you wish that your "volt" should be useful to you and if you do not wish to have all of your zeal in fabricating it come to nothing.

9. The correspondence between the subject for whom it is destined and the "volt" is obtained by a magical sexual operation, worked as we have described above, with, however, the following particularities.

After the usual seven-day preparation, as we have described, one should work sexually a single time, that is to say, on the eighth day only. But you will organize yourself in such a way that, on the day of your operation, the principal astrological force that presides over the horoscope of your subject should be in exaltation or, at least, in ascendance.

You will illuminate the room in which you will be working with the color of the subject's horoscope. You will determine this color according to the instructions given in this book.

During the first seven days of preparation you will exercise, by means of posism, the qualities of the subject that should be present to your spirit during the magical sexual operation of the eighth day.

You will make the gestures that characterize him; you will vividly imagine the penchants of his personality, in general.

At the end of the period of seven days, this man (or this woman) will be living in you, at the least evocation of your thought.

You will create the link between the "volt" and your subject by means of the exercises of volantia and decretism, to which you will devote yourself every day at the same hour during the week of your preparation.

The statuette that will be the "volt" must be placed in the room where you operate, in such a way that you may see it during the operational coitus.

For, once installed on the first day of preparation, it should not be touched again, or shifted, or have its place changed, until the end of the magical sexual operation.

When the operation of the eighth day is finished, you will put the "volt" back into the isolating vessel, and you will make sure that no one, except yourself, touches it.

Do not forget that if the "volt" is broken, the person to whom it is from then on bound by an unavoidable occult link dies at the same instant.

You have, thus, in your hands, the life and death of the person, which has been entrusted to you. You carry, therefore, a grave responsibility, and you must show yourself worthy of it.

Historical cases from the Middle Ages are told where this method served to remove many personages from the number of the living, having provoked the wrath of someone of power. In other eras closer to our own, the same method was used to accomplish assassinations, which remained unsolved by the authorities. In certain cases small wounds or prickings were found on the body of a deceased, whose death had no apparent cause, and no one thought of looking for the inhuman magician who amused himself by piercing with a needle or with the point of a knife the flesh, apparently inert, of the statuette, of which the *life* was magically linked to that of the deceased.

It would perhaps be right to hide such formidable possibilities of human power if one could truly hide them from all. But it is the same with this *power* as it is with any other deadly weapon: it is better to make it known to all, so that each may defend himself from it reasonably. True democracy is that which hides nothing from anyone.

10. To neutralize the "volt" and to annul its link with the subject, it is necessary to plunge it into water heated to 122 degrees Fahrenheit.

    For complete neutralization it is necessary that the statuette should remain in the hot bath for three whole days.

The temperature of the room should be stabilized at 60 degrees Fahrenheit.

11. Sometimes, though quite rarely, the three days prescribed do not suffice to completely suppress the effect of the "volt" on the subject. In such a case one should repeat the bath of the statuette one or two more times.

MAGICAL CHARGES

We know about the phenomenon of haunted houses.

We know that the life that goes on in a familiar interior engraves fluid images in the astral sphere, images that remain linked to the place and to the decor where they were born and that are there reproduced, either partially or completely, if the creative force of the long-gone personages was sufficiently powerful.

These images, or phantoms, reappear, habitually, independently of the will of those who perceive them; but one can also consciously provoke them, if their characteristic comprises affective elements able to stimulate human senses.

Initiates of all times have occupied themselves with this problem, and several among them have entrusted to their disciples methods permitting one to link whole scenes, or special forces, to the material chosen for this purpose.

Thus it is that certain ritual rings of the Middle Ages still conserve, in our own day, the fluid charges that were given to them centuries ago. A person putting such a ring on his finger would see in his dreaming absolutely authentic historical episodes: a rite, a banquet, a festival, a murder, and so forth.

These dreams are, generally, of a striking clearness, and on awaking one keeps the memory of them even to the slightest details.

When one knows the procedure, nothing is easier than realizing a magical charge; but the manner of doing it varies, according to its nature.

The three principal categories of magical charges are the following:

1. Planetary charges

    These serve to attract, or to obtain by induction, the planetary force desired.

    This preparation is subordinate to the time condition, which means that one will not realize it successfully except at certain determined times of the year.

2. Reproductive charges

    One makes them to re-create at will an image or a particular event. One is therefore bound, in this case, to the geographical condition of the place where the episode occurred.

3. Individual reproductive charges

    They differ from the preceding charges in this particularity, that they are destined for a certain person, in order to inform him or remind him of certain facts or certain persons.

    One will, consequently, have to take into account the individual birth chart of the person concerned.

    Charges of this category can be prepared to confer upon the person for whom they are destined the power to influence a third person, man or woman.

The objects chosen for these different magical charges may have any form whatsoever, and one may wear them as any kind of jewelry or talisman.

Fig. 15.1. Magical Ring—Model 1

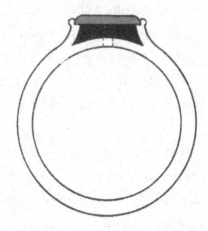

Fig. 15.2. Magical Ring—Model 2

But because the ring is the most usual form, we use it here, as an example, for the following instructions.

Rings that are destined to receive a magical charge always have three principal parts: a) the reservoir; b) the material with which one fills the reservoir; c) the precious stone or stones, chosen according to the individual horoscope.

When the stone indicated by the horoscope is transparent, one fashions the ring according to model 1, which has, besides the precious stone inlaid into the reservoir, two *fluorite* crystals sunken in hermetically and in such a way that they touch the liquid of the reservoir.

For a nontransparent stone, model 2 is more suitable, for it can directly touch the liquid, because light rays do not go through it.

But one should take care, in this case, to inlay the stone in such a way that there is no air passage into the reservoir, for it is absolutely necessary to avoid any possibility of evaporation of the liquid that fills it.

If it is a question of realizing a charge that needs several different precious stones, one should combine model 1 with model 2, by fixing the nontransparent stones in place of the crystals of model 1.*

But in all combinations that prevent the precious stone from directly touching the liquid of the reservoir, the fluorite crystals are indispensable.

The planetary charges and the reproductive charges, not being personal, can be worn, with the same success in their action, by anyone; but the personal charges do not function unless they are on the finger of the person for whom they were prepared.

Table 15.1, which is given below, will serve for charges of the first two categories.

---

*[The French text says "the crystals of model 2," which is incorrect. —*Trans.*]

Table 15.1. Combined Planetary Influences

	☉	☽	☿	♀	♂	♃	♄
☉	active sexuality authority	idyllic dispositions	practical and idealistic orientation	sensuality and sentimentality	love of glory; calm, courage	altruism	creative imagination
☽	favorable combination; harmony	imaginative sense of justice	force of concentration	light and changeable love	rapid and unstable enthusiasm	fickle fantasy	passive submission to astral influences
☿	favorable combination; strong intelligence	favorable combination; idealism, poetry	calm, practical commerce	love of mystery	oratorical talent, search for the unknown	wandering, undirected thought	intuition; love of the "beyond"
♀	favorable combination; understanding of sexual mystery	favorable combination; intelligence, mental curiosity	favorable combination; pronounced aesthetic sense	passive sexuality; benefic influence	good resistance to the difficulties of life	love of nature; seeking after the mysteries	succubic and incubic loves; sabbat
♂	favorable combination; energy, courage	unfavorable combination; instability of ideas	favorable combination; mental combativeness	unfavorable combination; warlike dispositions	active sexuality; erotic tendencies, aggressive tendencies	love of order; connected thought	hate, rage, wickedness
♃	favorable combination; beneficial ambition	favorable combination; dominating strength	unfavorable combination; licentiousness, thoughtlessness	favorable combination; sense of organization	favorable combination; activity, energy, intelligence	musically inclined enterprising spirit	understanding of symbols
♄	unfavorable combination; inability to submit to orders	unfavorable combination; lack of energy, laziness	favorable combination; diversified ingenuity	unfavorable combination; frequent nervous depression	unfavorable combination; nervous animosity	favorable combination; wisdom, philosophy	abstract thought, love for metaphysics

One will find, at the right, indications concerning the reproductive charges, and, at the left, those that pertain to the planetary charges.

At the same time, do not forget that the quality of action of the charge is closely linked to the mental force developed during the preparation of the jewelry.

16

SPECIAL CONDITIONS FOR THE PREPARATION OF PLANETARY CHARGES

1. The planetary charges envisaged in the preceding chapter have, for their goal, the accentuation or reinforcement of a given faculty in the person for whom the fluid condenser is prepared. That is why one does not charge the latter with two different planetary forces.

   But, if we wish to combine in the same person the forces indicated in table 15.1, below the line of separation of its two parts, we will prepare two pieces of jewelry for our subject, for example two rings, which we will charge respectively, each with its corresponding planetary force.

   Thus, if we wish to give to our subject energy and courage, and at the same time calmness and coolness, we shall fabricate on the one hand a solar ring, and on the other a ring of Mars. He will put both on his finger.

2. The planetary ring will be prepared according to the model that we have described in the preceding chapter; but the metal chosen for the fabrication of the reservoir will need to correspond to the desired planet.

   For Mercury, one will prepare a composite, formed of the six planetary metals, in equal parts.

   One will find the necessary instructions for this in table 9.1.

3. The precious stone chosen, it too according to table 9.1, will be inlaid in conformity with the instructions given in model 1, if it is transparent.

   One will work according to model 2 if the stone, determined according to the table, is not transparent.

4. One will contrive a small opening in the wall of the reservoir, so that the liquid fluid condenser may be introduced into it.

5. The reservoir, thus prepared, will need to remain in cold, running water for twenty-four hours.

   Immediately afterward it should be kept in the isolating vessel.

6. The liquid fluid condenser, which will be introduced into the reservoir, will need to contain one-third perfume of the corresponding planet.

7. One will charge the condenser with the desired planetary force in the same way as the "volts," after having hermetically sealed it in a quite clean vial and scrupulously observing the characteristic conditions with regard to color and perfume.

   The evocation of the planetary force itself will be prepared by means of the exercise of *posism*.

8. During the first sex-magic operation, which will immediately follow the period of preparation, one will charge with the desired planetary force the liquid blend, which is to be introduced into the reservoir right afterward.

   The opening contrived for the introduction of the liquid will then be blocked with solder.

   If the metal used for the fabrication of the reservoir can be amalgamated with mercury, one can make use of such amalgam for the solder.

9. During the second sex-magic operation and the following ones, one will charge the completely fabricated jewelry.

10. In devoting oneself to these various operations, one should take care to be aware of the placement of the constellations and the planetary aspects; for one cannot effectively charge jewelry and talismans unless the planet whose force one is evoking is exalted, rising, or, at the least, in a good aspect.

11. When the charge is sufficient, one deposits the jewelry into the isolating vessel and keeps it carefully to make use of it when needed.

All the work related to the preparation of a fluid condenser, including the operation of the mixing of the metals, indicated in step 2 of this chapter, must be performed by artificial light of the color corresponding to the planetary force to be evoked.

In the intervals between the various operations, the elements that will compose the jewelry or magical talisman will need to remain in the shade. For one must not forget that the light of day, and even that of the moon, cancels, partially or totally, the power of the planetary charges, opposing them with their different fluids.

17

SPECIAL CONDITIONS FOR THE PREPARATION OF PROJECTING CHARGES

We call "projecting charges" those that have the virtue of reproducing, in sleep or in the waking state, in the form of individual or collective visions, scenes or episodes whose imprint is engraved, as we have said, in the astral plane.

One prepares them according to the same method used for planetary charges, with the single difference that here the combinations of several planetary influences can be harmonized within the same object (a ring, a broach, or something else), provided that one conforms to the indications given in figure 15.2, upper half.

In this case, one does not only mix the perfumes of the different planets selected but also the corresponding metals and minerals that one will make use of for the fabrication of the reservoir.

To combine two different forces in one and the same fluid charge, one should first prepare the mixture of perfumes, observing the ratios indicated.

This mixture will immediately be combined with the fluid condenser, in equal parts, that is to say, one part of the mixture of perfumes to one part of the fluid condenser.

The greatest difficulty that presents itself to the operator in the course of the fabrication projecting charges consists in the posism and tirauclairism exercises, which must be perfectly executed to obtain good results.

We recommend, consequently, to all students with little experience, to abstain as long as possible from these experiments, for which even very strong posists and tirauclairists must prepare themselves for several weeks, re-studying certain principles that are indispensable to the success of the final operation.

It is good, in any case, to progress slowly, and in the beginning to make only charges projecting scenery: a landscape, an interior, a public square, and so forth.

Later, one should try to get simple scenes, and, when this becomes easily successful, one may give oneself more difficult tasks.

During the preparatory exercises and the charging operations themselves (the sex-magic working), it would be good to have a picture in the laboratory, reproducing the scene that is to be bound to the condenser.

The title of the scene, which one should prepare with the greatest of care, will need to be learned by heart, so that it may be perfectly engraved in the memory of the operator, at the moment of magical connection with the woman.

It is essentially recommended to not begin the active charging operation until the scene in question is so well fixed in the mind of the operator that the latter is able to reproduce it in his imagination, as a living tableau, at will and without the least fatigue or agitation.

That is also how one may recognize the good implantation of a given theme in the memory of an individual: a lesson well learned is easily evoked.

It is also absolutely necessary to know the exact stellar positioning of the two planets of which one proposes to receive the force: only work when the two forces are well aspected, that is to say, having a positive influence.

Do not forget to illuminate your laboratory, during the preparatory exercises and the definitive operations, with a combined shade of the two respective colors corresponding to your planets.

A few moments before the first sex-magic operation, add to the liquid fluid condenser, duly prepared, a drop of blood taken from the monthly discharge of your collaborator.

This drop is to be kept in the vessel until this moment.

Fluid-projecting condensers have formidable power, if they are well and exactly prepared.

On the finger of a medium or a sensitive person, the magical ring provokes a vision of the scene with which it has been charged, even if the person is awake.

In strong individuals, without mediumistic dispositions, the scene is reproduced in a dream, with such vital force and clarity of detail that in awaking from it they believe that they have really lived it.

The hidden and magical art that we teach has been cultivated with remarkable success in the Brotherhood of Eulis.

In 1871 one of our Brothers had prepared, in London, a fluid condenser in the form of a ring, which he put on the finger of a man condemned to death, on the day of his execution.

Two months later the ring was sent to Boston, where a person who knew nothing of the execution but who had the ring on his finger was able to recount, in front of a large audience, the whole scene, down to its smallest details, and with extraordinary exactitude.

On another occasion, the effect produced by a ring, magically charged with a stirring scene, was so strong that it was necessary to resort to an opposite suggestion to free the medium from obsession with the image, which had made the greatest impression on him.

INDIVIDUAL fLUID CONDENSERS

To prepare an individual fluid condenser, one establishes in the beginning the respective values of the planetary strengths and weaknesses, as revealed in the birth chart of the person concerned.

One generally ascertains, then, an obvious predominance of one of the planets over all the others, from its much higher numerical index.

Other forces are found, on the other hand, to be weak or even often to have a negative sign.

For the operator it is a matter of filling in these blanks by means of the fluid condenser, which, in attracting to the subject the planetary influences that he is missing, will accentuate and augment those qualities in which he is weak.

The horoscope of an ideally balanced person would give the same numerical index for all planetary influences.

Expressed in colors, such a horoscope would show a disk divided into seven equal parts and having within it all of the planetary colors.

But the individual, thus influenced, would not have any preponderant ability, and his life would go on in an awful monotone, bringing him nothing original or interesting.

This monster of balance would have no possibility of concentrating upon any kind of problem for longer than he would need to in order to maintain his physical existence; he would not, therefore, ever develop in himself a mental current likely to lead him to wider horizons. He would be a mediocrity, a man of brief emotions and flat aspirations, without passions or special characteristics. He would evoke neither fear nor love in anyone, and he would give the world nothing remarkable.

Let us not obtain for anyone who should entrust himself to us such a monstrous balance. Let reign over each the force that dominates him, and let us not intervene except where the accentuation of a too-weak faculty could be useful, without harming the originality of his nature. Let us remember well that the horoscopes of geniuses are, often, the most catastrophic.

And anyway, the operator, even the most able, will never essentially modify the specific character of his subject, for what he shall be able to attract to him, by means of the fluid condenser, will never be equivalent to a direct planetary influence through the birth chart.

What we will be able to do is to correct, to augment, to ameliorate, and that is already a lot. A weak memory can be strengthened, an unsteady health can be improved, an exaggerated misfortune attenuated.

But, quite often, to obtain the desired result, it will be necessary to resort to the simultaneous exercise of will, of suggestion, and even of posism, for the action of the jewelry to be really effective.

The preparation of planetary charges having been already sufficiently described in the preceding chapters, we shall limit ourselves here to pointing out the particularities concerning the personal charges exclusively.

1. For the fabrication of the reservoir, one should choose the metal corresponding to the planetary force that dominates the natal horoscope.

    The precious stones and the content of the reservoir should be selected in precise agreement with the numerical index of the different secondary planets figuring in the same horoscope.

2. One should add the fluid condenser to the mixture that will fill the reservoir in the ratio of 10:1.

3. One should proceed to the charging of the condenser when the planet whose force one wishes to receive is well aspected.

It goes without saying that individual planetary charges can only be of use for the person whose horoscope has been consulted in the course of the different operations of fabrication.

Still, the owner of the magical jewelry will be able to use it, in certain cases, to influence, according to his wish, a person of another sex.

PART IV

Magic Mirrors

19

MAGICAL MIRRORS

THEORY

Many occultists of our day no longer believe in the possibility of seeing, in the magical mirror, personages and scenes evoked by the magician.

They have lost this ancient faith, because their talents and their insufficient knowledge have not permitted them to find, in the attempted experiment, confirmation of the fact, which is, nonetheless, real.

In vain, the celebrated Dr. Dee of London, and quite a few others before him, have made use, for this type of seeing, of a concave mirror, of glazed carbon, and of still other things, to attract the image or the idea from the higher planes that they could not receive in any other way. The materialist era cannot admit that a simple physical coefficient, such as the oval concave mirror, a crystal, or a drop of ink, could drag out of a spirit that which the latter guards jealously in its impenetrable depths. The materialist era needs a material proof within reach of all. We shall make an effort to provide it here.

We don't doubt that the Christian dogma of immortality of the soul is in agreement with the truth.*

A thousand things prove it to us, and we believe in it, as we believe that the power that caused the world to exist is stronger than the rocks of the sea.

Certainly there have been some true mediums in the world, and there are some still, who know how to put themselves in contact with souls that have disappeared, but the innumerable theories of heartless people, of tricksters who dream only of filling their pockets with gold robbed from credulous dunces, have hidden the occultists behind a throng of madmen.

Lies have discredited the truth, and today the public is tired of the spiritualism that has been offered to it, because it takes too much patience to discover its plundered treasures.

Today's occultists babble at random. They do little.

But some serious work and some conscientious experiments can rehabilitate the traditional knowledge of the ancients. We are convinced of it, and we shall attempt to do it.

The spiritualism of our ancestors had in-depth knowledge of the secrets of the magic mirror.

The *Urim* and *Thummim,*[†1] polished surfaces of all kinds, served

---

*[This is Randolph speaking; Naglowska did doubt it and had already ceased to believe it. —*Trans.*]

†[Naglowska wrote, "Urim et Thumin," and her final "-in" instead of "-im" in the second word corresponds to a typographical error on p. 45 of the printed edition of Randolph's *Seership! The Magnetic Mirror.* This obviously suggests that she had the printed edition. We shall see other evidence, though, that may be suggestive of a handwritten document (perhaps his original manuscript, which may have already contained the error in the Hebrew word and misled his printer). Randolph

for religious seeing, for warnings, and advice asked of the gods.

Zoroaster was already preaching the magic mirror. After him, Socrates, Plotinus, Porphyry, Iamblichus, Chichus, Scaliger, Cardanus, have praised its virtues. Later still, it was the turn of Robert Fludd and of the great magician and recognized clairvoyant Paracelsus.*

We could cite more than three thousand names of grand masters versed in these mysteries, and some among them are still living.

The secret of the magic mirror is a few steps away from our region of shadows. A very short road separates us from it, but its pole is lost in the Infinite, and it itself is here, down below, up above, everywhere.†

Everywhere, except in the dark hole where we confine ourselves.‡

In the earlier time of our pagan ancestors the mountain lakes, fed incessantly by the pure water of streams, were, generally, the preferred places for magical manifestations.

(cont'd) said that the Urim and Thummim were polished breastplates, but most scholars believe they were things put into the high priest's breastplate. Naglowska is more noncommittal, saying, "polished surfaces of all kinds." Here, and in the following section, we can learn a lot about Naglowska's methods by comparing her source in Randolph to her "translation." The latter is, as will be seen, more of a paraphrase, hitting the high points, and it (thankfully) leaves out much that would be of little interest to the modern reader. —*Trans.*]

*[For those wishing to follow along, this section begins about mid-page on p. 46 of *Seership! The Magnetic Mirror.* —*Trans.*]

†[This remarkable passage is a paraphrase of an equally remarkable, but somewhat different, one by Randolph. He wrote (*Seership! The Magnetic Mirror,* p. 46): "The plane of the mirror is before us, within so few feet or inches; but its lanes lead down the ages, and its roads up the starry steeps of the Infinite. Its field is the Vastness below, within, above, and around and elsewhere; but that elsewhere contains all life next off this life is an immortal factness . . ." Clearly, what Naglowska was doing was rewriting Randolph's book—and I think for the better. —*Trans.*]

‡[This statement has no corresponding one in Randolph and is pure Naglowska. —*Trans.*]

We find the memory of it in fairy stories, which speak to us of the forests of Laynchork, in Craic-pol-nain; of Devil's Glen, in County Wicklow; of the Sorcerers' Mountain of Italy; of the famous Babia Gora (the Mountain of the Woman), on the border between Poland and Slovakia.*

Tacitus[†] spoke of lakes and water sources of this type, found on the plains of Germany.

But what is still more interesting, for a person of modern education, is Lane's work, titled *Modern Egypt*.[‡]

Lane was a skeptic who wanted to see with his own eyes the boasted experiments of an Egyptian magician of his time.

The magician in question generally began his operations by writing formulas of evocation on six scraps of white paper, which put him in communication with the spirits. After that, he brought a metal plate, full of small bits of burning wood charcoal, and had a young boy approach him.

---

*[I was not able to identify most of these places, but County Wicklow is in Ireland, just south of Dublin. Naglowska wrote Laynchork as Laynchark, which may suggest a handwritten manuscript (which of course could be hers, rather than Randolph's). Similarly, she wrote Craic-pol-nain as Craicpol-main. Randolph's handwriting was pretty bad (see the inscription under his photograph near the beginning of this book), and it would have been easy to mistake an "o" for an "a" or to confuse "m" with "n." Randolph had placed Babia Gora "between Hungary and Poland," which is at least imprecise, because those two countries are separated by Slovakia. Naglowska placed it correctly, on the border between Poland and Slovakia. She, familiar with Slavic languages, also provided the gloss, and the statement that it was "famous." —*Trans.*]

†[Naglowska wrote this name as "Facius," which strongly suggests a handwritten manuscript. —*Trans.*]

‡[The actual title of this work by William Edward Lane is *An Account of the Manners and Customs of the Modern Egyptians, Written in Egypt during the years 1833, 34, and 35, Partly from notes made during a former visit to that country in the years 1825, 26, 27, and 28!* The book was an instantaneous success, and the first edition sold out within two weeks. It was reprinted many times during Randolph's lifetime, and it is still available today in print-on-demand editions. —*Trans.*]

To Lane's question as to who are those who can see into the magic mirror, the magician responded: "The young boy who has not reached the age of puberty, the virgin, the black female slave, and the pregnant woman."

To be sure that the boy who was called to the séance would not have been influenced in advance by the magician, Lane sent his valet, asking him to bring the first child of male sex that he found on the road.

When everything was ready and the boy had been brought, the magician threw a piece of incense and one of the six scraps of paper onto the burning charcoal.

He then took the hand of the boy and drew a square surrounded by some mysterious signs on his palm. After that, he placed the little magic mirror in the middle of the square and ordered the boy to stare at it without turning his head away.

The lad obeyed and said several minutes later that he successively saw a man sleeping,* seven men carrying flags, an army busy setting up tents, and finally, numerous eager servants around the Sultan.

Lane tells, as follows, what happened then:

"The magician turned toward me, asking me if I wished to see a person who was absent or dead.

"I named Lord Nelson.

"The young boy whom we had made come there had never heard this name, and he had trouble pronouncing it. The magician ordered him to say to the Sultan, 'My master sends you his best remembrance and asks you to present Lord Nelson to me. Present him before my eyes, so that I may see him quite easily.'

---

*[In Randolph's printed original, the man is sweeping, not sleeping. —*Trans.*]

"When the boy had pronounced this formula, the desired vision was undoubtedly realized, for he added at once, 'Another man has just arrived. He is dressed in a black outfit (Lord Nelson always wore dark blue clothes), in European style. This man doesn't have his left arm.'

"Two minutes later, having seen more clearly, he corrected himself: 'No, this man does have his left arm, but he has it attached to his chest.'

"It is well known that Lord Nelson, who had lost his right forearm as a result of an accident, always wore his empty sleeve fastened to his chest.

"I then asked the magician to tell me if the mirror reflected objects as do ordinary mirrors. He answered that the law of reflection was the same for both types of mirrors.

"I had to agree, then, that the boy's description truly corresponded to that of the real Lord Nelson.

"But this experiment, although convincing, was not enough to banish my skepticism forever, because some other experiments, done in my presence, had produced no results; perhaps because of certain English friends of mine, who hadn't been able to keep from laughing during those séances.

"I gave myself up to the reality of supernatural phenomena on the day that a boy, called to look into the magic mirror, gave, upon request of a member of the audience, an exact description of his father, whom the boy had certainly never seen. Also, none of us except our friend knew the gentleman.

"The boy gave the following description: 'It's a gentleman, dressed in the style of France. He is holding his head in his two hands. He is wearing glasses. One of his feet is on the ground, while the other is raised behind him, as if he were getting down from invisible chair that he had been standing on.'

"It was extraordinary! The son of the gentleman evoked told us that his father actually did often put his hands to his temples, because he suffered from continual headaches. One of his legs was constantly bent back, as the boy had seen, because of a problem with his knee, left over from a fall from a horse while he was hunting.

"At another séance, equally interesting, we were given a perfect description of Shakespeare, and I could well have given other examples where a magician's knowledge had amazed a large audience, composed mostly of English skeptics."

Our readers could profitably compare these lines, written by Lane, with similar descriptions given by Kinglake in his remarkable work, *Eothen*.*

It is interesting to note that at a certain hydromantic experiment, made within our brotherhood, the young boy of whom we were making use for the experiment, saw better without the help of the medium.

He was able to distinguish strange images in a bucket of water. One might have believed that his own imaginings were being reflected in the water.

But we would like to look more deeply into this problem.

We would like to explain how these things are possible, and why modern humanity rejects them and persistently mocks them.

A multitude of questions, then, presents itself to our mind:

---

*[Naglowska spelled this book title *Tothen*. The book, which concerns the travels of the author, Alexander W. Kinglake, in the Middle East, has been reprinted many times and is widely and cheaply available. —*Trans.*]

From whence comes the imagination, which, from the brain of an individual, projects itself upon a polished surface and is there reflected, immediately, in a way that is perceptible to human eyes?

Are there, perhaps, in space, unknown beings who form a sort of invisible public around us? A public that may even be mocking us?

Or rather, is life nothing more than a routine mechanism, a harmony of matter, which scientists will explain to us one day?

Do miracles exist?

Do the souls that leave this world return to it again?

What is chance?

Can we know the future?

From whence comes the fear of the marvelous that reigns in humanity?

Why are there always some people who are persuaded of the existence of ghosts?

How does it happen that history, science, and "common sense" do not band together among themselves to knock down spiritualist beliefs forever, to erase them, so that they definitively give place to the "reality" of the positivists?

Can't humanity free itself, once and for all, of all "illusory monsters"?

Couldn't it say no to the fear and courageously confront the beings from beyond the tomb that present themselves to it in the form of impalpable visions?

Nothing serious will be done by mankind in this domain as long as light has not illuminated the shadows.

Man will not be at home on this earth as long as the unknown parades itself around here in that way.

But he won't chase away the unknown, and he won't make a peaceable guest of it, as long as he has not conquered within himself the fear of this unknown, which places itself in front of him like a door that cannot be entered.

For—and I repeat it—it is the fear, it is the terror of the supernatural that prevents our heroism from blossoming and from confidently approaching the mystery.

Fear is a heavy cloud that draws to us our desire for security, but which, in its turn, attracts us, and it is thus that we would like our life to be a dream and for the "beyond," where those who have left us already are, to be, instead, the reality.

We ask ourselves: Where are our dead? Where will we ourselves go? Those who have disappeared, are they still around us? Will we see them again someday?

I answer *yes* to these questions, and I attest that the beginning of this knowledge comes, like an unexpected flood, on the shore of the body and the soul.

But men, instead of receiving the knowledge, to increase and develop it, veil the fear that seizes them then, with the mask of obstinacy and a skeptical smile.

In society, Man is courageous; but alone, he falls back into the clutches of fear.

Often, an experience persuades him, a reassuring hypothesis calms him; he gets his courage back while listening to something a friend says, in which he would like to believe.

But there it is! He would only like to, but he cannot believe, for the modern era forbids that which it cannot accept using the habitual methods. And the modern era recognizes no superstitions!

Does not recognize them? It is, then, full of them!

Man is curious by nature. He likes to know the truth; he seeks it always, everywhere.

But he wants truth to be proved to him by experience, by experience accessible to his five senses.

Oh! He would certainly believe, if he could!

But manifestations of paranormal phenomena are so fantastic, so contrary to the logic of habitual human reason that he prefers to content himself with normal scientific laws.

Man says to himself: the root of the mystery is the lack of positive data; if I dug deeper, the secret would disappear and give way to understanding.

Man is right, in saying that, but unfortunately he does not do as he says: he contents himself with knowing only a little.

Modern man pretends to study nature, but in reality he looks into nothing but the material. Modern science makes no in-depth effort.

But superficial knowledge does not suffice except for light conversation, conversation that consists in making jokes.

Our brotherhood makes a different effort. On a ladder of a thousand steps, we slowly climb toward the higher regions, where the central meaning of life is found.

We build the bridge of understanding that is lacking to the majority of our contemporaries, and, with the help of this bridge, we transport ourselves to the other bank, where we collect the precious pearls that they cannot gather who have no hands.

We reverse the reign of cowardice, the rules of half-belief, of faith mixed with doubt.

We laugh at the writer who, faced with the marvelous, concludes that it is impossible.*

We blush with shame for him when we hear him cry superstition where he *half sees,* but cannot *reach,* because of his limited senses; and we shudder with indignation when we see him describe splendid things, the smile on his lips, that comical smile that hides his fear of being taken seriously . . .

We affirm this: superstition debases the person who is little evolved, but it refines the strong soul.

Walter Scott, who claimed to be an unbeliever, defended, and even adored, the superstitions of the common people.

But he made the mistake of explaining them. He explained and re-explained so much that the miraculous in them disappeared.

And Walter Scott, himself, really seems to have lost the truth in this dangerous game.

Will we ever get to the point of establishing clearly that truth, although it is only *our* truth, can be accessible to all?

Was the mental horizon of Walter Scott too limited to embrace the impalpable?

We can't bring ourselves to admit that he really may have doubted the existence of the invisible.

It is more reasonable, it seems to us, to suppose that he veiled his knowledge of the mystery, to adapt himself to the romantic style of his time. He wanted to charm his readers.

Perhaps he also wished to seem "wise," under the cloak of comic affectation. In this case the cloak must have been for his public and his real faith for himself.

---

*[In this section, Randolph was quoting Kinglake; Naglowska has, in turn, simplified and paraphrased what Randolph wrote. —*Trans.*]

Many other writers have done the same. They smiled, while speaking of the mystery, to follow the fashion, to please the public. Behind their comical grimace, the fear of *what will people say?* is visible . . .

People, in general, are too unsure in their beliefs. In the face of normality (*of the majority*), they rarely have the strength to be themselves. Custom dictates form to thought, just as it dictates to us the style of the clothes we wear. We fear the world's criticism . . .

But, I'll tell you this: the writer who hesitates to illuminate the supernatural with its true light, would do better not to occupy himself with it at all.

If one believes, if one has reasons to believe, one must confess one's faith, one must say what one knows . . .

And it is not necessary to overexplain supernatural phenomena.

For, by explaining, one complicates, and that is when sublime things become really incomprehensible.

The artificial explanation falls too easily into pieces, and, when it has fallen, the truth no longer survives. Besides, haven't we noticed that scientific explanations don't persuade anyone? Those who already believe, perhaps. But the others?

An uncomfortable fact is noted, it is not accepted. And if inner conviction refuses it, one claims trickery, charlatanism.

The world is made this way: the reasoning of others does not persuade, and, if fashion enters into it, each one believes that he doesn't believe.

Every new fact, every new proof that comes down to us, is labeled as black magic . . . Black magic? Horror!

But if the new idea is *comfortable,* if it corresponds to the human interest, a simple label is sufficient to defend it . . . Obviously, since one accepts it right away . . .

Within our confraternity, we have been, we are, and we shall always be partisans of clear and strong reason, of human reason.

One easily understands that most spiritual phenomena can be explained by the theory according to which the powerful magnetism of the universe may be forced, by the medium or, more strongly still, by the void, to reflect itself, that is to form waves in the opposite direction, as does the circle, formed on the surface of the water by a pebble's fall.

The reflected magnetic circle has no will of its own or any possibility of choice in its orientation. It is subject, in its development, to a precise law of direction; and laws, still unknown, transform it into movement upon the invisible surfaces. So may it be. We are willing.

We even admit that one may discover, in the points where different magnetic circles cross, the root of all the attractions and all the repulsions that we call sympathies and antipathies, in any supernatural phenomenon.

But, if we accept this explanation for the birth of phantoms, which are only a microscopic and useless part of the secondary nature of humans, we affirm, at the same time, that real phantoms are something else.

What? Our contemporaries are not trying to find this out, for the detached entities of all who are living do not interest them.

One discusses it inconclusively, without really wanting to know, and we are where we were: in ignorance.

We reject these vain discussions, and we put the following simple questions to modern science:

Do ghosts exist?

Do humans have other ways of knowing than their five normal senses?

Do phantoms have need of a body to manifest?

Does spiritual life go beyond material life, or not?

We could go on thus for a long time, but all the answers we would get would always come down to this: matter is everything, and there is nothing, or almost nothing, outside of it.

This sentence does not satisfy us in any way; for, if the five human senses teach us everything that we can know, if matter is all of nature, if blind chance is the king of the world, if we are alone in the universe, without direction or supreme plan, if there is nothing, anywhere, except what scientists can demonstrate to us, if human reason, although limited, is infallible and human *good sense* is the only initiator, if what the materialist tells us is the whole truth, the only truth—then, it would be better to immediately abandon all the mysteries and forever reject all spiritualist "superstitions," which haunt us and frighten us.

We could then more quickly root out the supernatural, which would then be nothing but a vain amusement, and life would be easier, existence surer.

Why torment ourselves, if nothing exists up there? Are we children, to amuse ourselves with childish games? Why fear what doesn't exist?

Is it reasonable, is it worthy of mature people, to let ourselves be made fools of by fairy stories invented by some tricksters for their profit?

The scientists are the kings of our time; it is they who decree in this sensory world.

They are our leaders! Oh yes!

Comical leaders, for one cannot have faith in them!

They leave us on the ground. They sit us down, each in our corner, and introduce machines into our souls. They turn us into mechanics, and they abandon us. We march in place, that's all.

The near-sighted eyes of the materialists do not see the *invisible,* which is why we call it such.

The *other* plane does not exist for them. They cannot pierce the veil that separates the material from the spiritual.

Ah! Yes! Let us salute materialist science, but, first, let us take away from it all hope for a future. Let us also take away from it too much care for the present.

Let us leave it in peace, in peace.

Real magic—that which the "experts" will never know—rests on the knowledge of the deepest and most secret forces of the mental plane.

Normally, our spiritual nature is imprisoned within us. We are not acquainted with it. That is where the saying of the sage comes in, "Know thyself."

Spiritual miracles are nothing other than the miracle of the opening of the mind.

One will find in vital magnetism the key of future magical science, which will unveil all the secrets of the creative spirit.

Magic is the great secret wisdom, of which all are ignorant. Reason is the formidable error, which all admire.

Man parades his reason, which he creates himself.

Materialism accepts it, because that is what has brought mankind out of its childhood. Man has become Man because of his reason, and he is proud of that.

Magic, although infinitely wiser and truer, is rejected, as fraud and lying, because it *annuls Man,* as Paracelsus said. Magic proves to Man that he amounts to little within a whole that is immense.

And, of course, we are not forgetting the dishonest clairvoyants, who make use of the crystal ball or the magic mirror to give false prophecies to young women in love, telling them what they want to hear, to collect their change.

This is seen often, indeed, but there is no magic there at all. Didn't God give reason to both the good and the bad? Would you conclude that reason, in itself, is bad?

In New York, hairdressers often make use of pages torn from Bibles to dry their knives and their scissors. Would you say that the Bible is made for that?

One even sees, in this country, suitcases lined with Bible pages, but this Book was written for the elevation of the soul.

We agree that mesmerism sometimes disturbs the nervous system. But mesmerism is not all of magic. Seeing in the magic mirror does not have this problem, and the things that one sees there, the personages, the episodes, the symbols, are reflected with exactitude, cleanly, almost palpably, even when they are presented as a series of scenes. One sees them as one would any image in a normal photographic apparatus.

The magic mirror does not demand of the operator an abnormal state. Everyone who looks into the magic mirror has his senses intact. The brain is not thereby fatigued, and the nerves remain calm.

During mesmeric experiments, the images arise and disappear rapidly. The magic mirror, on the other hand, retains them as long as one wishes. Almost everyone can successfully use this method of clairvoyance.

There are several types of magic mirrors.

We have, first of all, the crystal; for example, polished coal.

But, one doesn't see many mirrors of this type, because it is very difficult to find a piece of coal that is sufficiently hard, smooth, and without any fissure, so that it can be polished suitably.

At the same time, such a magic mirror, when it has been made, is excellent. It attracts and conserves well the magnetic fluids that issue from the eyes of the operator and form, precisely, the perceptible image.

Note well that the image in question is not formed on the surface or even within the matter of the mirror itself, but at a height of a few millimeters.

This means that the fluid rays are reflected, that is to say, returned, before their arrival upon the surface of the mirror.

We prefer seeing by means of the magic mirror to mesmeric operations, because the latter require a sympathetic rapport* between the medium and the operator, without which one cannot obtain the clear vision of the images and ideas projected by the mind of the medium, as an objective reality of the exterior world.

It is true that spiritual magnetism, which one makes use of in mesmeric séances, does not easily project the product of the medium's pure fantasy or that of the operator, and that, consequently, the image perceived may really be an objective reality of the mental plane; but, on the other hand, how is one to know if what one takes, in these cases, for spiritual exaltation is not a simple simulation?

---

*[Randolph: "a necessary and unget-rid-of-able *rapport*" —*Trans.*]

Quite often, mesmeric visions are nothing but the fallacious product of the will or of the influence of persons present at the séance, or even simply the effect of a morbid state of the nerves and the brain of the medium. They could also be—why not?—a farce mounted by some inhabitant of the other planes.*

The medium, himself, cannot reassure us on this subject, for, by definition, he is only an instrument, a machine, influenced by a force of which he is unaware.

He moves, speaks, and acts, as an unconscious automaton.

If one reflects upon all of this, one must agree with us that the magic-mirror sight is much more positive.

We group, into a second category, the magic mirrors that are prepared according to strict scientific laws.

We there distinguish, first of all, rules pertaining to the form and established after numerous well-controlled experiments.

A strange observation has to be made here. It has been noted that cutting a skull horizontally and exactly above the ears gives, for all heads, absolutely the same oval; while the human brain, seen beneath this cut, corresponds perfectly to the form of the terrestrial globe.

There has been an effort to adopt this form for the magic mirror, and it has been determined that it is the best.

Indeed, the oval thus obtained gives two foci, placed with mathematical precision, always the same.

The magnetic current, emitted by the posterior surface of the brain, falls upon one of the foci, it is reflected, and it runs around the brain toward the other focus, forming the magnetic circuit,

---

*[Randolph: "a transcript from the playful fancy of a disembodied wag or experimenter" —*Trans.*]

which then excites the anterior part of the brain, that which is in contact with the two corresponding foci of the mirror.

In this way, the magnetic force, put into play, is advantageously activated by the movement of the facets of the brain, excited by the current.*

Numerous experiments have proven that a good magnetic mirror is not dependent only upon its shape. The material of which it is made plays an equally important role in giving it all its necessary qualities.

We have seen, for example, that in the case of a flat mirror surface, the magnetic current, in being reflected, magnetizes only the anterior part of the brain of the observer, for the rest of the fluid is lost in space, after having gone through the mirror.

In certain experimental lodges, numerous chemical trials have been done with a view to finding a material likely to stop the loss of the magnetic fluid, which is, as we know, excessively fine.

Insulating materials have indeed been found; but even with the best of these compounds, the concave form shows itself to be insufficient, for it allows the fluid to slip off, which then disappears like a soap bubble.

The convex form presents another problem. The invisible ball of the magnetic aura remains attached beneath the mirror, and consequently loses its action upon the observer.

After long groping for a way forward, one has come back to the concave form, but with the following improvements.

---

*[Randolph: ". . . by reason of its increased magnetic play and motion of the brain-particles there situate" —*Trans.*]

1. The edge of the mirror is protected by a frame of fine gold, fashioned according to the laws governing fine liquids and gases.

2. The insulating material is chosen according to its electrical, chemical, and magnetic affinity with the mental magnetic fluid.*

Obviously, this requires extreme skill and ability.

Right away it was determined that the electrical insulating materials are completely transparent to the magnetic fluid.

One tried lithium, sodium, and different alkaline metals and even ammonium, but all of that was without result.

The alkaline clays of magnesium, barium, strontium showed themselves to be similarly insufficient, and the same goes for cerium, lanthanum, zirconium, tellurium, beryllium, thorium, yttrium, and aluminum.

One turned then to the metals that form, upon oxidizing, natrium,† copper, uranium, lead, cobalt, zinc, nickel, cadmium, bismuth, iron, chromium, and manganese.

All of this, too, was as ineffective as a basket used to capture the rays of the sun.

Compounds made with arsenic, tin, osmium, niobium, antimony, titanium, molybdenum, and tantalum, gave materials quite close to what we were looking for, but we still wanted to try the precious

---

*[Randolph: ". . . elective, electric and chemical and magnetic affinity to and with the finest form of magnetism known to science and to human experience" —*Trans.*]

†[Natrium is the Latin name for sodium (symbol Na), which has already been mentioned above. It was not mentioned here or anywhere under the Latin name by Randolph. Perhaps (Na)glowska was just testing our attention. —*Trans.*]

metals, such as rhodium, ruthenium, silver, platinum, iridium, mercury, palladium, and gold.

One also examined the effect of sulfur, selenium, chlorine, phosphorus, fluorine, iodine, and bromine.

Some of these materials were able to be used with a certain amount of success, when one added to them oxygen, hydrogen, carbon, boron, wax, or glass.*

Two of these compositions, mixed with paranaphthalene, finally gave the desired material, that is to say, a composition that was strongly electrical and very fine, as it must be to give to the surface of the mirror all its magical properties . . .

The man who limits his curiosity to the things of practical life is a blind shell, tossed by the waves of the sea.

He ignores the treasures that surround his small and narrow world, and he doesn't see the marvelous summits hidden in the depths of the waters that rock him.

He doesn't know that beyond our material world, above and below, there are other innumerable worlds. They are as incalculable as the stars of the nighttime sky.

Man, confined in his narrow shell, does not know, because he does not wish to know, that often dream, which is another intense life, gives us a slight glimpse of the great Reality that is hidden from us, and that mesmeric paths, which permit us to cross certain guarded borders, open before us astonishing depths where bits of the Universal Mystery are hidden . . .

Chance does not exist. Our mistaken senses have caused us to

---

*[The last two items were not mentioned by Randolph in the printed edition. —*Trans.*]

believe in it. When, by magic, we cast off the veil that obscures our view, we discover there, at the end of the wide, unknown road, the nothingness of this belief.

For there, the past, the future, and the present unite in a single interlacing, and one sees only a single eternal instant, where everything exists at the same time: what is, what will be, and what has been—a single unity that is present, complex, and incommunicable in a language limited by time and space.

The man who casts off the veil of obscurity sees this unique and eternal instant, and it is not difficult for him, then, to anticipate the future: he reads it as if on a written page.

For the Divine, time does not exist, and the illuminated man sees the Divine in its eternal and total presence.

But one cannot understand that, if one does not wish to be anything other than *normal.*

Sir David Brewster,* in spite of his will to interpret this truth in a vulgar manner, writes: "It is beyond doubt that, in the pagan temples, the gods of antiquity were at first invoked by means of the magic mirror."

In Tarsus, Esculapius had already said the same thing.

In the temple of Enguinum, in Sicily, the goddesses manifested themselves when evoked by the priests; and Iamblichus tells us that they appeared in the smoke, as if coming out of the fire.

We know how the magician Maximus[†] amused himself to frighten his guests, by making the statue of Hekate laugh.

---

*[Sir David Brewster (1781–1868) was a leading physical scientist of his day. His main interest was optics, but he also published a book titled *Lectures on Natural Magic,* which was addressed to Sir Walter Scott. —*Trans.*]

†[Lived ca. 345–420 CE. —*Trans.*]

Damascius, in a celebrated page, cited by Salverte*, says this:

During the evocation, we saw, firstly, upon the wall of the temple, a mass of light that seemed to come from afar. As it came closer, its form became clearer, and we distinguished, finally, a face animated by an angered look. This face was very beautiful and illuminated by a great intelligence. Faithful to their religion, the people of Alexandria adored this apparition, recognizing in it Osiris or Adonis.[2]

The king of Macedonia, Basil, mourning the death of his son, went to Theodore Santabaron, the well-known magician, and begged him to show him the deceased. The sorcerer, proceeding as was his

---

*[Anne Joseph Eusèbe Baconnière Salverte (1771–1839), usually referred to as Eusèbe Salverte. His 1843 book on the occult sciences[3] was translated from French to English and published, in 1846, as *The Occult Sciences, the philosophy of magic, prodigies and apparent miracles*.[4] Here is the quotation from Damascius, as found in the 1846 English translation of Salverte: "In a manifestation which must not be revealed . . . there appeared on the wall of the temple a diffusive mass of light, which in becoming concentrated, assumed the appearance of a face evidently divine and supernatural, severe of aspect, but with a touch of gentleness, and very beautiful to look upon. According to the dictation of their mysterious religion, the Alexandrians honoured it as Osiris and Adonis."[5]

And here is the quotation as Randolph reports it in *Seership!*: "In a manifestation (the cause of which, that is, a magic mirror, ought not to be revealed), . . . there appeared on the wall of the temple a mass of light, which at first seemed to be very remote; it transformed itself, in coming nearer, *into a face evidently divine* and supernatural, of severe aspect, but mixed with gentleness, and extremely beautiful. According to the institutions of a mysterious religion the Alexandrians honored it as Osiris and Adonis."[6]

Here is what Salverte originally said in French (published in 1843):

Dans une manifestation qu'on ne doit pas révéler il apparaît, sur la paroi du temple, une masse de lumière qui semble d'abord être éloignée; elle se transforme, comme en se resserrant, en un visage évidemment divin et surnaturel, d'un aspect sévère mais mêléde douceur, et très beau à voir. Suivant les ensei

habit, made him see the young man, luxuriously dressed, astride a splendid charger. The son bent down toward his father, embraced him, and disappeared.

This strange phenomenon was not due to charlatanism, for, even today, our perfected optical science is unable to imitate it. It is certain that Theodore Santabaron made use of a magic mirror, to give King Basil this exceptional consolation.

In his work consecrated to Benvenuto Cellini, Roscoe, in telling the adventures of the great artist, occupied himself with his evocations, realized by means of magic ritual, and it is interesting to note that neither Roscoe nor Brewster nor Smith believed that they were purely the product of artistic fantasy.

It is true that they try to discard the deductions that naturally present themselves in favor of our thesis, but they do it in such a clumsy way that their materialist suppositions do not persuade anyone.

One reads, for example, in Roscoe, that these astonishing phenomena were without doubt produced with the aid of a magic lantern, when everyone knows that Benvenuto Cellini lived in the sixteenth century, that is to say, a hundred years before the invention of Kircher's machine.

Further, what Brewster wrote on page 154 of his *Magic,* is so naive that it would be a waste of time to occupy oneself with it.

---

gnemens d'une religion mystérieuse, les Alexandrins l'honorent comme Osiris et Adonis.[7]

[What is interesting to me in all of this is that the source of Randolph's English was Salvert's original French, not the English translation. This is seen clearly in the mention of the apparition at first appearing to be remote (which is missing from the English translation of Salverte), and in Randolph's close adherence to the wording of the French original. It is very likely, therefore, that Randolph was able to speak and read French. —*Trans.*]

But, let us leave aside the question of charlatanism, which has always existed, and which will not disappear until the light shines everywhere. Let us come back to serious things.

The spiritual world has spoken sufficiently for one to be able to believe in it.

But, obviously, it is not the ordinary eye that distinguishes psychic and physical objects and phenomena, reflected by the magic mirror, but a special interior sense, which exists in everyone, and which must be developed, because in the ordinary man it is atrophied.

This special sense attracts to the ordinary eye the image of the supranormal apparition.

The spiritual being that inhabits the physical person possesses numerous unknown senses, which form the root of our five exterior senses and give us our different capacities.

For us, therefore, it is a question of establishing a bridge, a link, between our exterior and interior senses.

This bridge will permit us to escape from the prison of the material world and to penetrate into the etheric planes.

Oh! You will understand one day that, if death is a passive state in the physical kingdom, it is, on the contrary, an active blooming in the mental kingdom.

But the duty of the living person is to find the life and activity of the mental plane, without becoming physically passive.

Our school teaches our students penetration into the higher spheres, without losing view of the earth and the laws that govern it.

That is why we recommend experiments done with the aid of the magic mirror.

Plato said the phantom is the image of reality, living in the interior light.

The magic mirror attracts the form of this reality, fixes it, and reflects it, according to exact psychic and physical laws.

The interior light reflected by the magic mirror joins in the normal human eye with the exterior light, and there produces the sensual phenomenon of the vision. But if the interior light is not joined to the exterior light, we remain in pure imagination, not made concrete.

The interior light, when it is isolated from the exterior world, reposes in a calm and clear atmosphere.

This calm and this clarity persist when the exterior manifestation is produced.

It is the peaceful light of which ancient and modern books speak.

It is the peaceful light of which Zoroaster and the other sages and wise men of the East speak.

He who knows the invisible does not use haste, or empty small talk, or useless anger.

His soul is peaceful. Silently and patiently, he waits for his faith to open for him the doors of the Mystery.

To be sure, it is not necessary to discuss too much or to explain in minute detail the different methods of evocation.

One can discover all of that oneself, without too much instruction, but it is also certain that perfumes and magnetic vapors have always been of great help for seers.

Hundreds of persons have visited the rooms of the Fraternity of Eulis on Boylston Street in Boston.

All of them have been surprised by the calm that reigns in our midst and by the tranquil assurance permeating our Brothers.

Everyone keeps quiet and waits patiently for perfumes to be scattered and incense burned.

A penetrating music makes itself heard shortly thereafter, and, slowly, clouds of vapor arise from the tripods.

With their caress they shade the marvelous mirror, prepared for the experiment.

Faith in the reality of the supernatural is the only means for cleansing souls of cold and obstinately blind atheism.

When this essential verity is understood, the whole world will have a different attitude toward magical phenomena.

Through this book we would like to cut the imaginary knot by which people believe themselves to be irremediably attached to a single exterior universe.

We do not wish to reinforce superstitions, but we would like to give back to the supernatural the throne that has been taken from it.

TECHNIQUE

If you would like to make use of the magic mirror, do not forget the following rules.

1. The mirror must not be touched by anyone except its owner, in order to avoid mixing a stranger's magnetism, which could cancel that by which the mirror has been charged.

Other persons may look at it, but they must not touch either the frame or the surface of the mirror.

2. If the mirror is dulled, one can remove the dust with soap.

   One should wash it immediately afterward with alcohol, and when the mirror is dry, one should rub it again with fluoric acid, and then polish it with velvet or chamois.

3. Every day, for five whole minutes, one should magnetize the mirror with the right hand.

4. Immediately afterward, one should refine the action of the mirror's surface by means of magnetic passes made with the left hand.

5. The more often and the longer one uses a magnetic mirror, the better, for the action of the mirror grows with use.

6. To fall asleep with the aid of the magnetic mirror, it is necessary to stare at its center, calmly and without the least troubling of spirit. The visions appear, then, in dreams.

7. It is not necessary for the shiny surface of the mirror to be struck by the sun's rays, which paralyze the magical action. In using the mirror, keep its back to the window.

8. The magic mirror should be held at an angle, like a book.

9. If several persons wish to see at the same time, fasten the mirror to the wall, and let no one touch it!

10. The best position for seeing into the magic mirror is that which allows no reflection of ambient light.

    So look for this position, tilting the mirror in every direction, until its surface is like a single sheet of water: dark, smooth, and clear.

When the magnetism coming out of your eyes shall have accumulated above the mirror (a few millimeters from its surface), the limpid water will give place to the desired vision.

11. One will see, first, clouds of various colors.

    These clouds will seem to form in the material of the mirror itself, but that is only an optical illusion. In reality, the magnetism is concentrated above that.

12. Brunette persons with dark eyes and with a magnetic temperament charge the mirror more quickly, but not more strongly than blonds with their electric temperament.

    Generally, one can say that men do not see as easily as women, but when they see, they distinguish the details better and are less troubled.

13. At any rate, it has been proved that young boys and girls who have not reached the age of puberty see the most quickly and the most clearly, because their magnetism is pure and not sexualized. Purity is, as we know, a potent factor for all magnetic and occult work.

14. The white clouds that are seen in the magic mirror are a good omen. The answer that they bring to the question posed has a positive value.

15. The black clouds are a warning sign. Their sense is negation.

16. The violet, green, and blue clouds are good.

17. The carmine red, bright orange, and yellow announce bad influences.

18. If you use the magic mirror with a view to influencing a person who is absent, evoke his image by the force of your will. When it is in front of you in the mirror, stare fixedly at it

and concentrate all your imagination upon it. Your influence will strike it infallibly, no matter where on the globe it is found.

But don't forget that you will undergo the counter-strike of whatever it is that you have sent him. Evil will be repaid to you with evil, and good with good.

19. Have patience when you consult the magic mirror. Some people see almost immediately, while others have to wait for a long time.

20. The surface of the mirror must not undergo any chemical or optical influence, and one must carefully preserve it from the light of the sun, for it is as sensitive as a photographic plate.

    Moonlight, on the other hand, is beneficial for it.

    Extreme heat and cold are harmful to it, for the exaggerated temperatures cancel its force.

21. Every vision that appears in the magic mirror to the left of the observer is the image of something real and concrete.

22. What manifests itself to the right is symbolic. It is necessary to interpret it according to the traditional significance of the symbols.

23. The clouds or shadows that rise in the magical vision are affirmative responses to the questions posed.

24. Clouds or shadows that descend are negative responses.

25. Shadows that go from left to right signal the presence of an occult intelligence.

26. Clouds that travel from right to left signify that the séance must be ended.

27. If, after long patience, the desired result is still awaited, it is

permitted to make use of excitation sand, of which we will speak later in a special chapter.

But this sand is dangerous for most people; it is necessary then to use it with prudence and as seldom as possible.

When the excitation sand has had its effect, it is necessary to continue the work without it.

THE INSTIGATING
SAND

The instigating sand, of which we make use for our magical experiments, is not a novelty.

One finds it in many recipes of the Middle Ages.

The sorcerers of that era made use of it, among other things, to take off for the sabbat celebrations.

Still, we have made some modifications to it, for the following reasons.

In the Middle Ages the instigating sand was prepared by the maceration of plants in human fat.

There was reason for this bizarre procedure, for experience has shown us that the various substances used penetrate much better into the operator's pores if the conductor spread on his skin is similar to that which is found under his skin.

The best results are obtained with the grease extracted from the sweat of the experimenter.

But in the face of the numerous difficulties of such a preparation, we have replaced human fat with animal fat, which we first leave for a long time in coarse kitchen salt, and which we wash, immediately afterward, in cold, running water.

We repeat this salting and washing five times, and immediately afterward we plunge our fat into a hot bath.

This bath must last six whole hours.

To the fat, thus treated beforehand, we immediately add for 100 grams of fat:

     40 grams of hashish
     50 grams of hyoscyamus (henbane)
     80 grams of pommes d'épis*
     20 grams of belladonna
   260 grams of hemp
     50 grams of garlic
     30 grams of sunflower seed
     60 grams of calamus
   250 grams of poppy flower
   100 grams of wheat flakes

When the mixture is quite dry, we strain it in such a way as to get a very fine sand, which we keep in a sealed jar. We use the instigating sand, thus prepared, one or two minutes before the experiment.

With this sand we rub the solar plexus, the beginning of the

---

*[I am not sure what is meant by "pommes d'épis." It could be "pommes d'épices," spiced apples, but Naglowska would never make such a spelling error. It could also be "pommes d'api," a type of small apple with one side red and the other green, known mostly from a French folk song. We cannot be guided by Randolph, because no source for this formula has yet been found in his writings. —*Trans.*]

neck, the hollows of the armpits and knees, the soles of the feet, and the palms of the hands.

When the magical operation is finished, we immediately wash ourselves in hot water, and we rub ourselves with some essence of alum and petroleum jelly.

21

THE DIFFERENT
MODELS OF
MAGIC MIRRORS

We distinguish four kinds of magic mirrors:*

1. The small, ordinary mirrors, which are only a quite vulgar imitation of the true, operative magic mirror
2. Feminine magic mirrors
3. Masculine magic mirrors
4. Scientific mirrors, prepared in conformance with all the laws that we have presented in the preceding pages of this book

---

*[This part of the book corresponds roughly to Randolph's section II on page 81 of *Seership!* But where Randolph distinguished three types of mirrors in *Seership!*, Naglowska distinguishes four (she has added the "scientific," or "special," mirrors). It is possible that a privately circulated edition of *Seership!* contained the extra details, but I have not seen it. —*Trans.*]

THE SMALL MIRRORS

These are philosophical toys, rather than real, operative instruments. They have one or two foci, but one sees nothing more there than smoke, fire, a few symbols and some shadows, because their magnetic surface is very weak and their focal points are not placed with the desired mathematical precision.

They are used by Gypsies who are not able to obtain a more accurate mirror.* The easiest small mirror to construct is that of Claude-Lorrain. One forms a bit of clay, about a half-foot square, giving it a slightly convex surface.

One allows it to dry, fires it, and polishes its convex surface, as well as one can.

After that, one pastes the hermetic cardboard to this surface, and one molds the corresponding concave form.

Between the two surfaces, convex and concave, one then pours liquid glass, and one fires the whole thing until the glass has taken, between the two forms, the desired curve.

One then immediately prepares, in the same way, a second glass and welds it to the first one, leaving an empty space of about a quarter of an inch between the two surfaces.

This empty space will be filled with black ink, through a small hole made for this purpose in the joining. The hole will be hermetically sealed when this operation is finished.

Another small mirror, quite widespread, is that of Dee of London.

One prepares it as follows:

---

*[Here ends the first extract from Randolph's public edition of *Seership!*, and the expansion of detail begins, continuing until the next footnote. —*Trans.*]

One chooses a very black piece of anthracite, large enough to get from it a cube of at least a half-foot.

One must be careful that the surface, which will be polished, has no fissure, nor the least gray spot.

One carefully hollows out this surface, in such a way that the desired concavity appears, between its diameter and its maximum depth, a ratio of 5 to 1, and one immediately polishes it, finely.

The mirror thus obtained must be surrounded with a hardwood frame.

Dee's mirror can be used by an observer operating all alone, but the results are better if one works with the help of a medium.

We rank in the same category of small, ordinary mirrors quite a few other magic mirrors employed by oriental wizards and sorcerers, of which one finds the description, for example, in Lane.

They are, for the most part, quite primitive mirrors, prepared with a material that does not concentrate very much magnetism, because the currents escape it or pass through it easily.

These mirrors can only be used if they are very small. If they exceed a half-foot in diameter, it is difficult to charge them magnetically.*

THE FEMININE MIRROR

This is a larger model than the preceding ones.

The seers give it the name "feminine mirror," or "mirror of

---

*[The first expansion of detail ends at this point, and we return to material that is found in the public edition of *Seership!* —*Trans.*]

the good sex," because its focus is situated with mathematical exactitude.

Well prepared, this mirror has a great force of magnetic attraction, as well as great sensitivity.

The magnetic layer remains a little flattened on its surface, but it is not necessary for its diameter to exceed eight inches.

The feminine mirror is as good as the masculine mirror for all experiments in magical seeing, but it does not have as great an ability to cast an influence upon an absent person, or to evoke their image.

For symbolic and panoramic* visions, it is completely sufficient.

As we have just said, its diameter is normally eight inches or a little less.

The feminine mirrors are quite widespread in the West.

One prepares them with the same materials as the masculine mirrors, of which we will give the description below, but in a smaller size, as we have seen.

Cases are cited where great extravagance has been lavished on the fabrication of feminine magic mirrors, in the hope of obtaining a more efficacious magic; but experience has proved to us that fabulous cost is not always accompanied by a more remarkable virtue.

Maharaja Dhulep-Sing,† for example, had three magic mirrors, of which one was made from an enormous diamond, the second from an immense ruby, and the third from the largest emerald in the world.

But all of that did not permit him to pass up, or even to attain,

---

*[Actually, Randolph had used a word he made up: "phantoramic." —Trans.]
†[This was "Dhuleep Singh" in Randolph. —*Trans.*]

the habitual results obtained by means of our mirrors, scientifically constructed of materials that were quite a bit less costly.

MASCULINE MIRRORS

These mirrors, much stronger and more effective than those of which we have just spoken, have an oval form, of 14 x 10 inches.

Their magnetic surface is enormous.

One makes use of them more often for the experiments that are called "commercial" than for operations of private interest, because they can show up to three different scenes at the same time to three observers.

They are especially well known in Louisiana and in Syria.*

The masculine magic mirror is made of glass, cut with precision and containing 1 percent fine gold.

Its varnishing is done at an astrologically propitious time, and all the operations concerned with its preparation are effected by yellow artificial light.

The varnishing mixture is composed of very fine powdered iron, silver bromide, lactucarium (of the carbon of atropa and belladonna leaves), and of cobalt oil, proportioned as follows:

For one part of powdered iron, three parts of silver bromide, two parts of carbon lactucarium, and seven parts of oil.

The magnetic surface of the masculine magic mirror is as sensitive as a photographic plate. If an unknown person holds the mirror in his hand, even if it be for only ten minutes, it reacts without fail several days later; and one then sees appear on its surface, which

---

*[Here ends another extract from *Seership!*, and an expansion of detail, not found in the public edition of that work, begins. —*Trans.*]

is normally absolutely black, numerous gray spots, symptom of a contrary magnetic charge. The effectiveness of the mirror will then obviously be lessened.

A masculine magic mirror, suitably cared for, can be used for a very long time.

SPECIAL MAGIC MIRRORS

Figure 22.1 gives us an exact image of the construction of the magic mirrors that are called *special*.

There are some variations of detail, according to the purpose that the mirror will serve. We distinguish four principal categories of this type of mirror.

1. Special magic mirrors, normal type
2. Special magic mirrors, planetary type
3. Special magic mirrors, individual type
4. Special magic mirrors with a living magnetic layer

To facilitate seeing in the special magic mirrors of the normal, planetary, and living layer types, one can make use of a counter-insulator, fixed above the mirror by means of three golden holders, separated from the periphery of the polished surface by a distance of from one centimeter to a centimeter and a half.

Even a student with little experience can construct this mir-

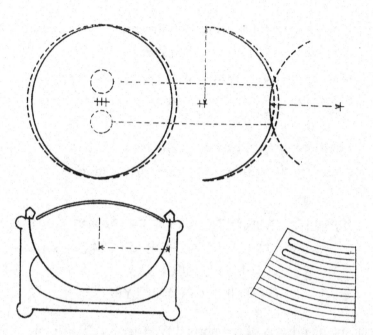

Fig. 22.1. The Construction of Magic Mirrors

ror, staying close to our design, which is why we do not give a more detailed description.

It remains understood, at the same time, that the student will work seriously and with all due attention.

The preparation of a special magic mirror requires the following conditions:

1. All materials used for its construction will be carefully freed of any foreign currents.
2. One will work, during its construction, by appropriate artificial light.
3. During its construction, one will keep the mirror completely isolated.

4. One will care for the finished mirror in such a way as to keep it always in its living magnetic state.

5. During the experiments, one will hold the mirror obliquely, like a book, with the two focal points lined up vertically.

The best proportions between *a* and *b* are 34 for *a* and 32 for *b*. But one can vary these dimensions, keeping the ratio.

SPECIAL CONDITIONS OF PREPARATION AND WORKING FOR SPECIAL MAGIC MIRRORS OF THE NORMAL TYPE

Special magic mirrors of the normal type are used when one is not familiar with the birth chart of the person concerned.

The layers of the surface, indicated in fig. 22.1, are composed as follows:

Layer *c* is of glass, containing 2 percent fine gold.

Layer *d* is a glaze of silk, prepared with the thread taken directly from the cocoon and reduced to a paste in clean water at 420 to 430 degrees Fahrenheit, under pressure. This paste, well dried, is ground to a powder, to which one adds, immediately, liquid gum arabic.

Layer *b* is the essential layer of the mirror. It is made up of one part silver amalgam, three parts powdered sulfur, seven parts carbonized vervain, one part phosphoric acid, and nine parts paranaphthalene. If necessary, the paranaphthalene can be replaced by potter's wax. The mixture thus obtained is spread over the mirror while still hot, in several layers, until a thickness of a quarter of an inch is reached.

Layer *a* is of fluorite, with a thickness of a sixth of an inch.

Glass, which as we know does not permit the passage of magnetic fluids, is only used as an insulator in the construction of magic mirrors.

In the absence of fluorite, one can use a plant varnish to make the concave surface of the mirror shine.

For the preparation of a special magic mirror of the normal type, one should choose the color of the lighting, the perfume, and the astrological epoch of Venus, but one does not create a sexual charge.

SPECIAL PREPARATION AND WORKING CONDITIONS FOR SPECIAL MAGIC MIRRORS OF THE PLANETARY TYPE

Special magic mirrors of the planetary type serve to attract forces, genies, and phantoms of the chosen planet.

Layer *f* is made of a silk varnish, prepared as indicated in the preceding chapter.

Layer *g* is glass mixed with pure gold.

Layer *e* is of porcelain.

Layer *d*, a seventh of an inch thick, is made of the metal that corresponds to the planetary force, chosen according to table 9.1.

Layer *c*, very fine, is of beeswax, boiled three times in very clean water. It will be magnetically charged, in accordance with the indications given in the preceding chapters.

Layer *b* is the essential layer of the planetary mirror. It contains, for one part of gold chloride, three parts sulfur, eleven parts carbon, product of the mixture of flowers that one will find by consulting the table of correspondences on the line of the chosen planet, two parts of the perfume of this same planet, one part of phosphoric acid, fifteen parts of paranaphthalene, three parts of boiled beeswax. The thickness of this layer must be a quarter of an inch.

For the preparation of a special magic mirror of the planetary type, one will choose the color of the lighting, the perfume, and the astrological time, according to the planet whose force one wishes to evoke, without any sexual charge.

SPECIAL PREPARATION AND WORKING CONDITIONS FOR SPECIAL MAGIC MIRRORS OF THE INDIVIDUAL TYPE

A special magic mirror of the individual type can only serve for the experiments of the person for which it has been made.

It is constructed according to the data of the birth chart of its proprietor.

The different layers of this type of mirror are the same as those of the planetary mirror.

Only the following particularities apply:

Layer *d* is made from a mixture of metals chosen according to the gradation of forces of the horoscope.

Layer *b*, which is the principal layer, will contain eighteen parts liquid fluid condenser, duly charged, one part powdered sulfur, five parts paranaphthalene, twelve parts individual perfume, six parts carbon, prepared with the same plants that were used for the individual perfume, half a part phosphoric acid, and one part of the blood of the person concerned.

The thickness of this layer should be a quarter of an inch.

The color of the lighting during the work, the perfume, and the astrological time are to be chosen in conformity to the birth chart.

There is no sexual charge.

Note: The special magic mirror of the individual type easily acquires the properties of a "volt." It must not therefore be entrusted to the hands of strangers. Only the owner of the mirror may touch it without danger.

To neutralize the mirror, leave it in cold, running water, for at least twenty-four hours.

SPECIAL PREPARATION AND WORKING CONDITIONS FOR SPECIAL MAGIC MIRRORS WITH LIVING MAGNETIC LAYERS

The special magic mirror with living magnetic layers contains the following layers:

Layer *a,* of fluorite;

Layer *h,* of silk varnish;

Layer *i,* of glass mixed with gold;

Layer *g,* of porcelain;

Layer *f,* of beeswax;

Layer *e,* prepared as in the case of the analogous layers of the individual type of the special mirrors;

Layer *b,* of varnish, composed of: fifteen parts of gelatin, six parts of the menstrual blood of the woman who is the working partner, two parts of her ordinary blood, one part charcoal prepared from her corneous substances, such as fingernails, hair, and so forth, ten parts pure water, four parts glycerin, one part liquid fluid condenser.

The liquid thus obtained must be hermetically sealed between two layers of fluorite, exactly aligned and soldered with the help of a gold amalgam.

The two layers of fluorite are to be separated one from the other at a distance of a third of an inch, and one should take care to evacuate the air before pouring in the liquid.

Without this precaution, the mirror will have no value.

Under the reservoir, which will contain the liquid in question, one must fix another layer of fluorite, also at a distance of a third of an inch.

In this new reservoir, one will introduce and hermetically seal, by means of the same gold-amalgam solder, the liquid of Mars, composed as follows:

For fifteen parts of gelatin, two parts of liquid fluid condenser, ten parts pure water, four parts glycerin, three parts sperm of the operator, and four-tenths of a part of his individual perfume.

When the mirror has been completely prepared, it is to be charged by means of the magical operation, as is done for the fluid charges described in this book.

During the operation, one is to vividly imagine that the two layers containing human blood awaken, becoming alive.

In addition, one is to abide by the following rules:

1. The woman with whom one works must have in her horoscope approximately the same constellations for the moon and Venus as the male operator.

2. The color of the lighting, the perfume, and the astrological time of the operation are to be determined by the horoscope data of the male operator.

3. The operation is to be done in working position number two.

   During the entire duration of this magical operation, one is not to remove the eyes from the surface of the mirror that is to be charged.

4. Once the operation is finished, one is to close up the mirror, not wasting a minute, in an insulating container, prepared in advance for this purpose, and the container is to be placed in the shade, in a place where daylight cannot penetrate.

Magic mirrors with living layers are the most efficacious and the most powerful of all those that have been build up to the present time.

At the same time, they have a drawback: their life is limited to barely fifteen months. Once this time is up, they suddenly become neutralized, as if by enchantment.

It is the sudden death of a living *thing!*

To keep a magic mirror with living layers in good condition, it is necessary to treat it very carefully and to use it at least once a week.

The charging of the two upper layers of such a mirror manifests clearly, some minutes after the beginning of the seeing operation.

It is rapidly accentuated, and if the observer is a very strong magnetizer, the mirror suddenly gives forth a light, in which is outlined the silhouette of the phantom.

Magic mirrors with living layers do not support a temperature that is above 78 degrees Fahrenheit, or below 68 degrees.

Daylight is disastrous for them, but the lunar rays vivify them.

LIVING TABLEAUX

U nder certain conditions, and with scrupulous accomplishment of the magical work, the principles of which will be given in this chapter, one can animate, that is to say, render truly alive, portraits and statues, with a view to influencing one or several senses of a particular man or woman.

The influence that one projects in this way may be mental or physical, it does not matter.

The doctrine of magically animated tableaux is not new. In the Middle Ages, certain painters knew it very well and applied it artfully; but one also mentions cases where the human magnetic fluid became concentrated of itself upon an old portrait, forgotten in the corner of a room of some feudal chateau, where, in the course of the monotonous years, scenes of violent passion took place.

One does not say as much of certain sacred paintings, done on the walls of Christian churches. They suddenly became animated, and worked real miracles.

Obviously, the will of the wise man, initiated into the mysteries of the great magical art, can do better and more surely than mere fortuitous adventure.

The wizards and sorcerers of past centuries knew this, and they studied the problem in depth.

They teach, in the writings that have been found, that a painting in poppy oil, in a golden frame, gives astonishing results, because the poppy oil is an excellent fluid condenser and the golden frame a perfect insulator.

Fixed to the wall of a church, where believing people often kneel, or hung from the silk tenting of a salon, where dreams and violent passions are exalted, an artistic work becomes, little by little, a true center of life, because the oil retains human currents, and the golden frame keeps them from escaping.

We are aware, as is everyone, that some charlatans and persons of bad faith have profited from this verified truth to gain money shamefully, fooling too-credulous clients; but what is true is true, nevertheless.

We possess, in our lodge, several authentic grimoires, which deal abundantly with this subject. When we read these old writings, it sometimes seems to us that the harsh eye of the real magic of the Male casts its terrifying gaze upon us.

We read, for example, in certain formulas, that a mixture of colors, to which has been added the blood of a fetus torn from the belly of its mother by the operation of the cross, is of surprising effectiveness.

Other formulas tell us that one gives formidable power to a living tableau if one mixes into its colors a few drops of blood of a pure virgin, offered after that to the pleasure of the succubus.

There are some drugs, recommended to painters, which contain a human magnetic charge, worked on the basis of solitary excitation. Their effect is particularly malefic. Human folly made use of them, in the dark ages, to perpetrate mysterious assassinations: an enemy, masked by the kindness of the gift offered sent death in the succubic tableau, and the person, beneficiary of the gift, who hung the portrait in their living room, died from it soon afterward.

The Holy Inquisition tried to put an end to these frightful abuses, burning the manuscripts of the wizards and persecuting the magicians. All magical science could have disappeared in the fierce reaction of Catholicism, but, fortunately for us and for the future of humanity, there were always some philosophers who were able to guard the secret and act under cover of the revengeful hand. Those cultivated the magical art for the good cause of initiatic knowledge.

So it is that one of our Brothers, who lived in Spain, in the first half of the eighteenth century, was able to recover some manuscripts containing formulas and advice of great importance.

That Brother devoted ten years of his life to this study and research.

He conscientiously subjected to experiment everything that he was able to find on the subject of the theory and the fabrication of living tableaux, and upon his death he left a testament to the Eulis Brotherhood, which contained marvelous formulas for the preparation of simple but powerful drugs, of which we still make use today.

In the course of his busy life, our Brother had himself also constructed some animated portraits, of which he gave us the key.

The benefic magical action that he was able to deploy brought such fame to him that the crowds constantly assailed his small cottage to ask him for advice and cures.

This Brother who was of such great merit was murdered by religious fanatics.

You may read below an extract of his testament, of which we have only suppressed a few passages that were too intimate.

EXTRACT OF THE TESTAMENT OF
OUR BROTHER CHARSAH

My long theoretical studies concerning living tableaux were at first unfruitful.

The rare tableaux that I succeeded in animating died quickly, and the phantoms that I called up did not have the faculties that I wished.

I varied my models, I tried the most powerful fluid condensers, but in vain: I did not obtain what I wanted.

But one day, thanks to a happy chance, I was able to ascertain that the son of one of our peasants, who every day made an ardent prayer in Spanish in front of an image of the Madonna, involuntarily became, through that, her succubus. I then had the solution I was looking for to the problem.

I went to the painter who had made this holy image, and I learned that the model who had served him for this painting was a courtesan of strong passions. The painter amused himself with her during his hours of rest, on a bed in his studio, in front of the easel.

The artist was not wealthy. To save the little money he had, he did not buy canvas for this tableau, ordered by the son of the peasant, but he painted it on a square that he cut from the sheet of his bed of love.

This detail struck me, and I had then, for the first time, the idea of the individual perfume. I then applied myself to seeking the formula for the drug, according to the data of the astrological correspondences. This was a difficult task, which kept me busy for several months. I spent a lot of time going over some old grimoires again, in which the essential things are hidden in floods of almost useless details. But having found the treasures of this antique science, I had no trouble with the rest of the work.

I soon persuaded myself that it was completely useless to make use of corneous substances such as hair and fingernails, for the debris of human flesh dies rapidly, and if one cannot replace it in the course of the work, all of one's trouble is in vain. Not to mention that, for the reconstruction of old paintings, these materials cannot be found, while the individual perfume can be prepared as well by a living person as by a person who is long since dead.

In exactly observing all the rules that we summarize below, one infallibly gets the phantom that one wishes. If the result is not correct, it is because there has been an error, either in the formula of the drug, in the astrological calculations, or in the drawing, or the expression, or the colors of the tableau. It is certain that the reconstruction of a living tableau according to the retrograde astrological chart, based on the proportional data of the portrait, is a work that requires great patience. In addition to the technical approach, it also requires a considerable initiatic sense, and this is not an art that one learns comfortably.

We recommend to the student who is not sufficiently sure of himself that he get the help of a psychologist.

In the art of reconstruction of living tableaux, it is necessary to distinguish four different cases.

a) The portrait done after a living model, the details of whose birth chart one knows;

b) The portrait done after the astrological details of an unknown person from the past, from the present, or from the future, of a particular race;

c) The portrait of a known person from the past or present;

d) The portrait, old or modern, already done, but which is to be re-animated.

Special conditions for each of the four cases mentioned

A) The portrait done after a living model, the details of whose birth chart one knows

1. One will first of all determine the rapport of the resulting forces in the birth chart and prepare, according to the data obtained, the individual perfume of the person in question, and the oil, which will serve for mixing the colors. Do not forget to macerate all plants used in boiling oil for at least two minutes.

2. The cloth used for canvas must be linen or hemp, but never silk. It is necessary to cut it in good dimensions, for a portrait of natural size.

3. Do the background of the painting first, which must be of the individual color of the model.

4. Use the oil prepared according to the indications of paragraph one only for the figure and the clothes.

5. When the tableau is dry, repeat the same figure on the back, but as a negative.

6. The contours of the figure that is painted on the back of the

tableau must be filled with fluid condenser. This work must be done by artificial light of the individual color of the model. From then on, one works all the time by this same light.

7. When the painting on the back of the tableau is dry, cover it with a living layer, prepared according to the indications given for magic mirrors.

8. The image thus obtained will be polished on glass containing gold or covered with a layer of amalgam, where the silver will have been replaced by gold. Immediately afterward, cover the negative with a tissue of natural silk.

9. Put the tableau into a heavily gilded frame.

B) The portrait done after the astrological details of an unknown person from the past, from the present, or from the future, of a particular race

The preparation of an animated portrait of an unknown person from the past, from the present, or from the future, of a determined race and in conformity to the astrological details of the birth chart, requires the same operations as we have already indicated for the preparation of a portrait after a living model, with the single difference that the proportions of the drawing and the expression of the face will be found according to the birth chart, which will also indicate the color of the hair and the eyes, the shade of the skin, and so forth.

This work cannot be accomplished except by an astrologer of the first order.

It is further necessary that the painter who gives himself a task of this comprehensiveness should be an experienced typologist and that he not let himself be influenced by any living model.

A great artist, a great typologist, and a great astrologer must come together in the same person to perfectly realize a work of this category.

C) The portrait of a known person from the past or present

One undertakes the preparation of a living portrait of a personage known from the past or from the present when one wishes to attract to himself, for himself, and for others the benefit of the person's direct influence.

One will then have on hand a few images reproducing the traits of the personage in question and will also consult his or her natal horoscope.

For a personage from the past, one will establish a retrograde horoscope, having recourse to typology, if the data available are insufficient. This task is equally difficult, but if one works with skill and patience, one necessarily succeeds.

D) The portrait, old or modern, already done, but which is to be re-animated

Reanimating a portrait from which the life has gone out is the most difficult of all those that we have envisaged up to now, for without changing anything about the painting already done, in this case it is a question of recharging the human magnetic fluids, according to the appropriate typo-astrological data, composing from them the elements of the charge according to the indications of table 15.1.

Some General Conditions for the Four Cases

1. The living tableau, prepared according to our methods, must be hung on the wall of a room, which is to be specially con-

secrated to it, and where no one will ever enter except the owner and the woman who will work with him.

This room is to be of at least 860 cubic feet. Its walls are to be painted with oil in the individual color of the personage shown on the canvas.

Each time that the owner comes to operate before this image, he is to illuminate the room with the individual color of the portrait.

One should take care to place a divan in front of the tableau, so that the operator may be comfortable and be able to fix his gaze on the features of the image without useless fatigue.

2. A lamp should be placed between the portrait and the divan.

This lamp, made of a metal corresponding astrologically to the idea predominant during the execution of the painting, will spread throughout the room the necessary vapors, scented with the individual perfume, prepared according to the horoscopic data of the portrait. The lamp in question will support, consequently, a vase of the same astrologically corresponding metal, and one is to pour into it clean water and a sufficient quantity of individual perfume.

3. The woman is to be introduced into the room when the vapors, in light and aromatic clouds, shall have sufficiently filled the atmosphere of the room to protect it from the magnetism, perhaps contrary, of the woman.

One is then to make magical sexual love with this woman, strongly imagining the gradual animation of the portrait, until its complete vitalization.

One must not turn away the eyes until the end of the operation.

4. If you strictly conform to all that we are here teaching, and if you do not forget to perfume your solar plexus, the beginning of your neck, the hollows of your armpits and the backs of your knees, the soles of your feet, and the palms of your hands with the individual perfume of the portrait, you will see, while you are comfortably seated on the divan beside your lover, the air of the room gradually darken until it reaches a deep black. The portrait will awaken in the shadows, and the body, painted on the cloth, will suddenly shudder. The arms and the legs in the portrait will make uncertain moves, as if to assure themselves of the reality of their life, then, slowly, the whole silhouette will detach itself from the frame to advance toward you.

You can then obtain what you wish, but do not forget that in that solemn instant you are crossing the threshold of the Unknown, while breaking down the doors of the Mystery. Any moral fault committed at this moment will not be forgiven you, and unhappiness will implacably follow you your whole life if you have relighted an extinguished force to make use of it carnally. Do not call to you an extinguished life except to receive its occult light. This purpose, only, is blessed. The returner will answer any sensible question and will inform you, if you wish, about terrestrial events during his previous life.

But, my Brothers, beware of succubi and incubi, who reflect your vices and your hidden desires. These wretches will charm you by their powerful and effective voluptuous-

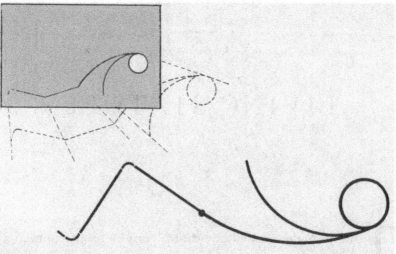

Fig. 23.1. Magical Coitus

ness, but you will irremediably become their slave. A minute of pleasure in the arms of a succubus is a pact signed with the Devil: all your life can be sucked out of you in a year.

It is your Brother Charsah who tells you all this before dying, for he has studied these things and now knows their mysteries.

LIVING STATUES

The principles stated above also permit the preparation of statues or other living sculptures.

One makes them hollow and of terra-cotta, most often.

They are fired when they are ready, and then bathed in the individual perfume, mixed with the fluid condenser.

This bath, which is produced by maceration, must last for twenty whole days.

Upon leaving the bath, the sculpture must dry for six days, at a normal temperature.

When it is completely dry, one gives it a layer of paint, with the colors prepared as for the tableaux.

The hollow space of the statue must be filled with the living liquid, whose recipe and manner of preparation have already been given.

The opening, through which one introduces the liquid, is to be sealed by means of a gold amalgam.

Plaster, wood, and porcelain are also materials recommended for this type of statue.

The materials indicated for the preparation of "volts" have also been used with success.

The well-prepared statue is to be placed on an insulating tray, at a distance of ten centimeters from a reflecting surface.

One will find all the other details, useful for this preparation, in table 9.1.

The magic of living sculptures was very popular in ancient Egypt, in Greece, and in the Indies, where even today one sees certain idols, haloed with gold and having an understandable purpose.

fINAL NOTE

The handwritten notes that have served for the arrangement of this book form the second part of the second degree of initiatic instruction, given by P. B. Randolph to the students of the Eulis Brotherhood.

They contain recipes for sexual magic on the basis of three elementary principles—mental concentration, astral correspondences, and the polarization of the sexes—with the help of which one creates, in the astral spheres, the corresponding forms, which attract the necessary forces for the realization of the desired phenomena.

Assuming that our readers have already studied the elements of astrology, or will do so by means of other books that treat of this science, we have only gathered here the details that are directly useful for experimental practice.

We have omitted a few recipes that are not necessary for sex magic, in order that persons who are insufficiently prepared should not experiment in vain with drugs and elements that are dangerous.

Sixty copies were made of Randolph's complete manuscript and entrusted to the Brothers of the Eulis Brotherhood for their personal use. It includes the following unpublished volumes.

FIRST DEGREE

Vol. I: The Ritual of the First Degree

Vol. II: Occult Theory, Orders, and Brotherhoods

Vol. III: Astrology: Minerals, Plants, Animals, Man, Sound, Word, Color, Perfume, Gesture

Vol. IV: Typo-Astrology and the Retrograde Reconstruction of Horoscopes

Vol. V: Occult Chemistry: Minerals, Plants, Animals, Man, Acoustics, and Optics

SECOND DEGREE

Vol. I: The Ritual of the Second Degree

Vol. II: Sexual Magic

Vol. III: Doctrine, Rites, and Symbols

Vol. IV: The Occult Mediumship and Alchemy of the Second Degree

Vol. V: Philosophical Summary of the Initiatic Rites of the First and Second Degrees

THIRD DEGREE

Vol. I: The Ritual of the Third Degree

Vol. II: The Philosopher's Stone

NOTES

FOREWORD. THE MOST INFLUENTIAL BOOK ABOUT SEX MAGIC EVER WRITTEN

1. Deveney and Rosemont, *Paschal Beverly Randolph,* 198–200.
2. Ibid., 27.
3. Ibid., 364.

CHAPTER 3. THE POLARIZATION OF THE SEXES

1. Deveney and Rosemont, *Paschal Beverly Randolph,* 361.

CHAPTER 10. MAGICAL SEXUAL OPERATIONS

1. Godwin, Chanel, and Deveney, *The Hermetic Brotherhood of Luxor.*
2. Randolph, *The Unveiling,* 17.

CHAPTER 19. MAGICAL MIRRORS

1. Randolph, *Seership!,* 45.
2. Ibid., 57.
3. Salverte, *Des sciences occultes.*
4. Salverte, *The Occult Sciences.*
5. Ibid., 281.
6. Randolph, *Seership!,* 57.
7. Salverte, *Des sciences occultes,* 216.

BIBLIOGRAPHY

Alexandrian, Sarane. *Les libérateurs de l'amour.* Paris: Éditions du Seuil, 1977.

Anel-Kham, B. (pseudonym of Henri Meslin). *Théorie et pratique de la magie sexuelle.* Paris: Librairie Astra, 1938.

Bardon, Franz. *Initiation Into Hermetics.* Salt Lake City: Merkur Publishing, 2005.

Deveney, John Patrick, and Franklin Rosemont. *Paschal Beverly Randolph: A Nineteenth-Century Black American Spiritualist.* Albany: SUNY Press, 1997.

Evola, Julius. *The Metaphysics of Sex.* New York: Inner Traditions International, 1983.

Geyraud, Pierre (pseudonym of l'Abbé Pierre Guyader). *Les petites églises de Paris.* Paris: Éditions Émile-Paul Frères, 1937.

Godwin, Joscelyn, Christian Chanel, and John P. Deveney. *The Hermetic Brotherhood of Luxor.* York Beach, Maine: Samuel Weiser, Inc., 1995.

Hakl, Hans Thomas. "Maria de Naglowska and the Confrérie de la Flèche d'Or." *Politica Hermetica* 20 (2006): 113–23.

Levi, Eliphas (Alphonse Louis Constant). *The Book of Splendours.* York Beach, Maine: Samuel Weiser, Inc., 1984.

Naglowska, Maria de. *La Lumière du sexe.* Paris: Éditions de la Flèche, 1932.

English edition: Traxler, Donald, trans. *The Light of Sex: Initiation, Magic, and Sacrament.* Rochester, Vt.: Inner Traditions, 2010.

———. *Le Mystère de la pendaison.* Paris: Éditions de la Flèche, 1934. English edition: Traxler, Donald, trans. *Advanced Sex Magic: The Hanging Mystery.* Rochester, Vt.: Inner Traditions, 2011.

———. *Le Rite sacré de l'amour magique: Aveu 26.1.* Paris: Supplement of *La Flèche Organe d'Action Magique,* 1932. English edition: Traxler, Donald, trans. *The Sacred Rite of Magical Love: A Ceremony of Word and Flesh.* Rochester, Vt.: Inner Traditions, 2012.

———. *La Flèche Organe d'Action Magique* 1–20 (Oct. 15, 1930–Jan. 15, 1935).

Péladan, Joséphin. *À Coeur perdu.* Paris: G. Édinger, 1888.

Pluquet, Marc. *La Sophiale: Maria de Naglowska, sa vie—son oeuvre.* Montpeyroux: Éditions Gouttelettes de Rosée, n.d.

Randolph, Paschal Beverly. *Eulis! The History of Love.* Toledo, Ohio: Randolph Publishing Co., 1874. [Health Research reprint, 1961.]

———. *Magia Sexualis.* Compiled and translated by Maria de Naglowska. Paris: Robert Télin. 1931.

———. *The New Mola! with Supplement.* Toledo, Ohio: Randolph Publishing Co., 1874. [Available as PDF from archive.org.]

———. *Seership! The Magnetic Mirror.* Toledo, Ohio: K. C. Randolph, Publisher, 1896. [Available as PDF from archive.org and as reprint from Kessinger Publishing.]

———. *The Unveiling: Or, What I Think of Spiritualism.* Newburyport: William H. Huse & Co., 1860. [Available as PDF from archive.org.]

———. *The Wonderful Story of Ravalette.* Boston: Randolph Publishing Co., 1871. [Available as PDF from archive.org.]

Salverte, Eusèbe. *Des sciences occultes ou, Essai sur la magie, les prodiges*

et les miracles. Paris: J.-B. Baillière, 1843. [Available as PDF from archive.org.]

———. *The Occult Sciences: The Philosophy of Magic, Prodigies and Apparent Miracles*. Translated by Anthony Todd Thomson. London: Richard Bentley, 1846. [Available as PDF from archive.org.]

Thimmy, René. *La Magie à Paris*. Paris: Les Éditions de France, 1934.

Vintras, Eugène. *L'Évangile Éternel*. London: Trubner & Co., 1857. [Nabu Reprint, 2010; PDF also available from archive.org.]

INDEX

Page numbers in *italics* represent illustrations.

BOOKS OF RELATED INTEREST

The Light of Sex
Initiation, Magic, and Sacrament
by Maria de Naglowska

Advanced Sex Magic
The Hanging Mystery Initiation
by Maria de Naglowska

The Sacred Rite of Magical Love
A Ceremony of Word and Flesh
by Maria de Naglowska

The Lost Art of Enochian Magic
Angels, Invocations, and the Secrets Revealed to Dr. John Dee
by John DeSalvo, Ph.D.

Introduction to Magic
Rituals and Practical Techniques for the Magus
by Julius Evola and the UR Group

The Morning of the Magicians
Secret Societies, Conspiracies, and Vanished Civilizations
by Louis Pauwels and Jacques Bergier

The Secret History of Western Sexual Mysticism
Sacred Practices and Spiritual Marriage
by Arthur Versluis

The Complete Illustrated Kama Sutra
Edited by Lance Dane

INNER TRADITIONS • BEAR & COMPANY
P.O. Box 388
Rochester, VT 05767
1-800-246-8648
www.InnerTraditions.com

Or contact your local bookseller